Intertribal Native American
Music in the United States

Intertribal Native American Music in the United States

∞

EXPERIENCING MUSIC, EXPRESSING CULTURE

∞

JOHN-CARLOS PEREA

San Francisco State University

New York   Oxford
OXFORD UNIVERSITY PRESS

Oxford University Press is a department of the University of Oxford.
It furthers the University's objective of excellence in research,
scholarship, and education by publishing worldwide.

Oxford   New York
Auckland   Cape Town   Dar es Salaam   Hong Kong   Karachi
Kuala Lumpur   Madrid   Melbourne   Mexico City   Nairobi
New Delhi   Shanghai   Taipei   Toronto

With offices in
Argentina   Austria   Brazil   Chile   Czech Republic   France   Greece
Guatemala   Hungary   Italy   Japan   Poland   Portugal   Singapore
South Korea   Switzerland   Thailand   Turkey   Ukraine   Vietnam

For titles covered by Section 112 of the US Higher Education Opportunity
Act, please visit www.oup.com/us/he for the latest information about
pricing and alternate formats.

Published by Oxford University Press
198 Madison Avenue, New York, NY 10016
www.oup.com

Oxford is a registered trademark of Oxford University Press

Library of Congress Cataloging-in-Publication Data

Perea, John-Carlos.
   Intertribal Native American music in the United States : experiencing music,
expressing culture / John-Carlos Perea, Ph.D.
      p. cm.—(Global Music Series)
   Includes bibliographical references and index.
   ISBN 978-0-19-976427-3
   1. Indians of North America—Music—History and criticism.   2. Music—United
States—History and criticism.   3. Indian musicians—United States.   I. Title.
ML3557.P47 2013
781.62'97073—dc23   2012043252

Printing number: 9 8 7 6 5 4 3

Printed in the United States of America
on acid-free paper

To my past:
Gertrude and John Mohr, Josephine and Carlos Perea,
and Bernard Hoehner.

To my present:
Jessica Bissett Perea, Barbara and Jacob Perea, Wilhelmina Phone,
the Perea and Bissett families, and all of the aunties, uncles,
and cousins who have invited me into their homes.

To the future:
Josephine Mary Bissett Perea and you, my reader.

Contents

Foreword   xi
Preface   xiii
CD Track List   xvii
Music Selections Available on Ping   xix
Illustrations   xxi
Maps   xxiii
Timeline of Songs and Events Referenced in the Text   xxvii

1. Thinking about Intertribal Native American Music   1
    Thinking about Soundings   4
    Thinking about Time: Past, Present, and
      Future   6
    Thinking about Intertribalism   8
    Thinking about Names and Terminology   10
    Introducing Myself: Where Are You From?   13
2. Sounding Communities: Intertribal Pow-wow Music   16
    Pow-wow Origin Stories   18
    Pow-wow Space   25
    The Role of a Singer   30
    What's Going On?   31
      Gourd Dance   31
      Grand Entry   32
      Flag Song   34
      Victory Song for Posting the Colors   36
      Intertribal Songs   37
      Contest Songs   38
      Other Social Dance Songs: Round Dance
        Songs   39

Honor Songs   42
Thinking about Dancing: Four Reflections
    on Pow-wow Dancing   43
    Michele Maas: Women's Jingle Dress   44
    Eddie Madril: Men's Fancy and Grass
        Dance   45
    Rulan Tangen: Women's Buckskin Dress   48
    Marcos Madril: Men's Northern
        Traditional   50
Thinking about Communities: Attending
    a Pow-wow   53

**3. Sounding Revitalization: Intertribal Native American
Flute Music   56**
Revisiting Names: Which Native American
    Flute?   57
Thinking about Revitalization   60
Native American Flute Origin Stories   61
Native American Flute Performers   63
    Doc Tate Nevaquaya   63
    Tom Mauchahty-Ware   65
    Kevin Locke   66
    R. Carlos Nakai   68
    Mary Youngblood   71

**4. Sounding Activism: Native American Popular Music and
the Occupation of Alcatraz Island   74**
Thinking about Alliances between Music and
    Activism   76
Red Power Origin Stories   76
Native American Popular Musicians of the 1960s
    and 1970s   80
    Peter La Farge   80
    Buffy Sainte-Marie   82
    Floyd Red Crow Westerman   84
    Redbone   86
    XIT   88

5. Sounding Unexpectedness: Native American Jazz Musicians 91

> A Brief Detour through *Rhythm on the Reservation* 92
>
> Unexpected Origin Stories: Native American Musicians in the Boarding School System 96
>
> Native American Jazz Musicians 98
>> Mildred Bailey 98
>> Russell "Big Chief" Moore 99
>> Oscar Pettiford 101
>> Jim Pepper 102
>
> Thinking about Unexpectedness 105

6. Epilogue: The 2012 GRAMMY® Category Restructuring and Future Definitions of Intertribal Native American Music 106

Glossary 111

References 117

Resources 122

Index 125

Foreword

ᗡᕐᗕ

In the past four decades interest in music around the world has surged, as evidenced in the proliferation of courses at the college level, the burgeoning "world music" market in the recording business, and the extent to which musical performance is evoked as a lure in the international tourist industry. This has encouraged an explosion in ethnomusicological research and publication, including production of reference works and textbooks. The original model for the "world music" course—if this is Tuesday, this must be Japan—has grown old, as has the format of textbooks for it, either a series of articles in single multiauthored volumes that subscribe to the idea of "a survey" and have created a canon of cultures for study, or single-authored studies purporting to cover world musics or ethnomusicology. The time came for a change and the Global Music Series is that change.

This Global Music Series offers instructors choices. Instructors can now design their own courses; choosing from a set of case study volumes, they can decide which and how much music they will teach. In addition, case studies offer two formats—some focused on a specific culture, some on a discrete geographical area. In either case, each volume offers greater depth than the usual survey. Themes significant in each instance guide the choice of music that is discussed and some of the themes occur in multiple case studies, contributing to depth and permitting comparative study. The contemporary musical situation is the point of departure in all the volumes, with historical information and traditions addressed as they elucidate the present. The framing volume, *Thinking Musically* (Wade), sets the stage for the case studies by introducing topics such as gender and globalization that recur in multiple volumes and other ways to think about how people make music meaningful and useful in their lives. *Thinking Musically* also presents the basic elements of music as they are practiced in musical systems around the world so that authors of each case study do not have to spend time explaining them and can delve immediately into the particular music. A second framing volume, *Teaching Music Globally* (Campbell), guides teachers in the use of *Thinking Musically* and the case studies.

The series subtitle, "Experiencing Music, Expressing Culture," also puts in the forefront the people who make music or in some other way experience it and also through it express shared culture. This resonance with global studies in such disciplines as history and anthropology, with their focus on processes and themes that permit cross-study, occasions the title of this Global Music Series.

Bonnie C. Wade
Patricia Shehan Campbell
General Editors

Preface

∞

The textbook you are holding in your hands is the product of a decade's worth of experience studying, teaching, and performing intertribal Native American music. That process began as a lecturer in American Indian Studies (AIS) at San Francisco State University (SFSU) in 2001. Having been hired to teach American Indian music six months after graduating from SFSU with my undergraduate degree in music, I turned to my own interests and experiences as a **musician** as a foundation from which to design the class. Since that time my research and teaching interests have centered on the four areas covered in this book: pow-wow music, Native American flute music, Native American popular music and political activism, and Native American jazz musicians.

In 2003, I was accepted into the graduate program in Music at the University of California, Berkeley, where I specialized in ethnomusicology and American Indian musics. One of the biggest and most rewarding questions I faced while attending graduate school was the question of how my identity as a Native American performer of Native American music could be seen as complicating my research and analysis. As Professor Richard Taruskin has written:

> I often get into interesting discussions with the ethnomusicology students at Berkeley when I question them on their frequent interest in studying the music of their own ethnic heritage. I call that "roots musicology" or (less patiently) "rootsicology" and I am skeptical of it, simply because to me the essential mark of a scholar is skepticism, while a sense of belonging breeds advocacy and a lowered critical guard (Taruskin 2009: 192).

It is relevant to recall Taruskin's skepticism—both of "rootiscologists" and the skepticism he foregrounds as necessary to scholarship—now because you are reading a textbook that is written from the basis of my research, interest, and participation in the music of my own "ethnic heritage." That being the case, the question in the process of thinking about and writing this book has been one of balance: How does a rootsicologist balance the needs of the objective eye and the subjective I? At this point I will not claim to have found the answer to what is an important but possibly unanswerable question. I have, however, found in ethnomusicology and in Native American Studies, my two parent disciplines, writings that provide a theoretical and methodological foundation for the present work.

In 2005, I was fortunate to meet Professor David McAllester (1916–2006) at a meeting of the Society for Ethnomusicology in Atlanta, Georgia. McAllester's writings on Diné (Navajo) music and **culture** were and are a major influence on me in terms of the way he represented the influence of intercultural relationships on the production of knowledge about music. The ethnomusicology faculty at Berkeley encouraged me to write to McAllester before the conference to arrange a meeting and he wrote back the following:

> Dear John-Carlos:
> Your letter was serendipitous. I had just written, in an article, that much of the future of American Indian ethnomusicology will be "homework" rather than "fieldwork," and in the hands of Native musicologists. We can lay the "ethno" to rest, or better still assume it refers to all of us. (McAllester 2005)

McAllester recognized that Native musicologists' continuing influence on the field of ethnomusicology would necessarily change concepts of how research is conducted. I choose to think of the present text as homework, not just because it creates a space for me to look at the music of my own heritage but because homework, for a teacher, is never complete.

This textbook is built upon a particular set of lived experiences and generational perspectives that inform my understanding of and teaching philosophy in relation to intertribal Native American musics in the United States. Those perspectives and practices are not fixed in time or space; they exist in a constant state of flux or coming into being. Therefore, if I position myself as a Native ethnomusicologist or "rootsicologist," I do so with the understanding that my homework will never end and any sense of expertise to be claimed from writing or reading this book exists only in relation to the commitment to see that the knowledge contained here is updated as it changes over time. The documentation of those changes is critical, not just to scholarship, but to the development of cultural and political solidarity that is based as much on respect for difference as it is an understanding of similarity.

McAllester's homework, then, allows me to position my responsibilities as a Native scholar in relation to my life and work. Taruskin's skepticism is addressed by means of self-reflexive engagement with the fields of intertribal Native American Music in the United States. But what about "knowledge" in all of this? What are you as the reader supposed to "get" from the experience of reading this book? Here I am influenced by the writings of curator and historian Paul Chaat Smith (Comanche). Discussing the innovative works of filmmaker Zacharias Kunuk (Inuit) and multimedia artist Erica Lord (Athabascan, Iñupiaq, Finnish, Swedish, English, Japanese), Smith states:

> At its best, this is what serious art practice is about: choosing the right questions and finding ways—visually, intellectually, emotionally—to explore them with viewers. It is not really about answering them. Often a successful investigation will not answer a single one, and instead raise new questions. (Smith 2009: 36)

In writing this book I find it useful to change "art practice" to "scholarship and teaching" in the above quotation and "viewers" to "readers and students." Given this newness of McAllester's homework as a conceptual model and my personal sense of it as a lifetime commitment, the idea here is not for you to passively consume knowledge. The idea here is to engage with processes of questioning not just what you know about Native American music but what you know about yourself in relation to Native American music. It is hoped that this textbook will offer as many questions as it does answers and, in doing so, will constructively contribute to the issues and continuing dialogues referenced here and in the following chapters.

ACKNOWLEDGMENTS

This book could not have been completed without support and encouragement from many aspects of my life. My parents, Barbara and Jacob Perea, set me on the path of being a teacher and have never stopped believing in my abilities. Dr. Bernard Hoehner gave me music and a life I could never have anticipated as a young man; I will always be grateful for him and my relationship with the Hoehner family. The departments of American Indian Studies and Music at San Francisco State University have played a major role in my teaching career and I am grateful for my teachers and colleagues: Joanne Barker, Ronald Caltabiano, Robert Collins, Clay Dumont, Andrew Jolivétte, Hafez Modirzadeh, Melissa Nelson, Elizabeth Parent, Roberto Rivera, and Dee Spencer. This book is also influenced by my graduate education at UC Berkeley and my experiences with Tom Biolsi, Ben Brinner, Jocelyne Guilbault, Pat Hilden, Richard Taruskin, and Bonnie C. Wade.

General editors Bonnie C. Wade and Patricia Sheehan Campbell provided consistent support and encouragement throughout the production of this text. I am also extremely grateful to Oxford University Press and my anonymous peer reviewers for their time spent developing the work.

The Office of Research and Sponsored Programs at SFSU provided course release and grant funds for music rights fees. Robert Doyle, Stephen Butler, Kristen Butler (Canyon Records), Tony Isaacs (Indian House), James Marienthal (Silver Wave), Cathy Carapella (Smithsonian Folkways), and Brooke Wentz (The Rights Workshop) worked with me on behalf of their respective labels and artists to provide the music on the accompanying compact disc. My American Indian music classes at SFSU and Stanford University provided a space to work on these ideas; I am especially grateful to students Randall Cunningham, Cassandra Freeman, CS Gomora, Stephen Kane, Rafael Moreno, Michaela Raikes, Ashley Richards, Moses Rodriguez, and Luke Taylor. Dirk Alphin generously shared his talents with Lakota font design and translation in chapters 3 and 4. Monica Magtoto (magtotoart.com) provided graphic design and technical assistance. My wife, Jessica Bissett Perea, gave unconditional love and support and my daughter, Josephine Mary, gave smiles, laughter, and a reason to keep going.

I am thankful for everyone who has contributed to this book by helping me learn, teach, perform, write about, and understand intertribal Native American music in the United States. Thank you!

CD Track List

1. Elk Soldier, "Hoka Hey" (excerpt). *A Soldier's Dream: Pow-wow Songs Recorded Live at Ft. Randall,* Canyon Records CR-6418, 2006.

2. Porcupine Singers, "Lakota National Anthem (Flag Song) and Veterans' Song." *Traditional Lakota Songs,* Canyon Records CR-8007, 1997 (originally recorded in 1978).

3. Kiowa Dance Group Singers [Bill Koomsa Sr. (lead singer), Billy Hunting Horse, Wilbur Kodaseet, Bill Koomsa Jr., Lonnie Tsotaddle, Georgia Dupoint, Ann Koomsa, Martha Koomsa Perez, and Pearl Woodward], "Kiowa Flag Song." *Kiowa: Traditional Kiowa Songs,* Canyon Records CR-6145, 1998 (originally recorded in 1975).

4. Black Lodge Singers, "Straight Intertribal." *Pow-wow Songs Recorded Live at White Swan,* Canyon Records CR-6273, 1996.

5. Young Bird, "Road Warrior." *Young Bird & The Boyz: Pow-wow Songs Recorded Live at Shakopee,* Canyon Records CR-6334, 2001.

6. Northern Cree, "Home of the Warriors." *Second Song…Dancers' Choice! Pow-wow Songs Recorded Live at Saddle Lake,* Canyon Records CR-6331, 2000.

7. Northern Cree, "Facebook Drama." *Dancerz Groove: Cree Round Dance Songs,* Canyon Records CR-6503, 2012.

8. Ironwood Singers, "Round Dance" (excerpt). *Sioux Songs,* Canyon Records CR-8030, 1978.

9. Ironwood Singers, "Little Bighorn Victory Song." *Sioux Songs,* Canyon Records CR-8030, 1978.

10. Doc Tate Nevaquaya, "Flute Wind Song Intro." *Comanche Flute Music Played by Doc Tate Nevaquaya,* Smithsonian Folkways Recordings SFW 50403, 2004 (originally released in 1979).

11. Doc Tate Nevaquaya, "Flute Wind Song." *Comanche Flute Music Played by Doc Tate Nevaquaya,* Smithsonian Folkways Recordings SFW 50403, 2004 (originally released in 1979).

12. Tom Mauchahty-Ware, "Courting Song." *Flute Songs of the Kiowa and Comanche*, Indian House IH 2512, 1978.

13. Kevin Locke, "The Photograph." *Love Songs of the Lakota Performed on Flute by Kevin Locke*, Indian House IH 4315, 1983.

14. R. Carlos Nakai, "Shaman's Call." *Earth Spirit*, Canyon Records CR-612, 1987.

15. R. Carlos Nakai, James DeMars, and the Canyon Symphony Orchestra, "Two World Concerto: Lake That Speaks." *Two World Concerto: The Music of James DeMars*, Canyon Records CR-7016, 1997.

16. Mary Youngblood "Beneath the Raven Moon." *Beneath the Raven Moon*, Silver Wave Records SD 931, 2002.

Music Selections Available on Ping

(https://c.itunes.apple.com/us/imix/intertribal-native-american/id553025235)

1. Belo Cozad, "Kiowa Story of the Flute." From *Library of Congress: A Treasury of Library of Congress Field Recordings*, Rounder Records.
2. Peter La Farge, "Custer." From *As Long as the Grass Shall Grow: Peter La Farge Sings of the Indians*, Smithsonian Folkways Recordings.
3. Buffy Sainte-Marie, "Now that the Buffalo's Gone." From *It's My Way*, Vanguard.
4. XIT, "End?" From *Plight of the Redman*, Sound of America Records.
5. Mildred Bailey, "Rockin' Chair." From *The Chronological Mildred Bailey, 1937–1938*, Classics.
6. Louis Armstrong and his All-Stars, "I Still Get Jealous." From *Hello, Dolly!* MCA.
7. Oscar Pettiford, "Stardust." From *Nonet and Octet*, Fresh Sound.
8. Jim Pepper, "Witchi Tia To." From *The Path*, Enja Records.
9. Jim Pepper, "Witchi Tai To." From *Afro Indian Blues*, PAO Records.

Illustrations

Map P.1.   Map of tribal areas in the United States (designed by Monica Magtoto, magtotoart.com).   xxiii

Map P.2.   Map of tribal areas in Alaska (designed by Monica Magtoto, magtotoart.com).   xxiv

Map P.3.   Map of tribal areas in Canada (designed by Monica Magtoto, magtotoart.com).   xxv

Figure 1.1.   Visual representation of linear time (designed by Monica Magtoto, magtotoart.com).   6

Figure 1.2.   Visual representation of circular time (designed by Monica Magtoto, magtotoart.com).   7

Figure 1.3.   Dr. Bernard Hoehner at Three Rivers Pow-wow, *c*.1980s. Photo courtesy of the Hoehner family.   15

Figure 2.1.   Northern Cree Singers, Saddle Lake Pow-wow, Saddle Lake First Nation, Alberta, Canada, 2011. Photo by Stephen Butler, courtesy of Canyon Records.   17

Figure 2.2.   Four circles of the pow-wow as described by Dr. Bernard Hoehner (designed by Monica Magtoto, magtotoart .com).   26

Figure 2.3.   Visual representations of Northern and Southern Plains pow-wow song forms (designed by Monica Magtoto, magtotoart.com).   33

Figure 2.4.   The Ironwood Singers, 1979. Photo courtesy of Canyon Records.   40

Figure 2.5.   Northern Cree Singers, Honoring Singers and Songmakers Round Dance, Louis Bull Reserve, Hobbema, Alberta, Canada, 2003. Photo by Stephen Butler, courtesy of Canyon Records.   41

Figure 2.6.   Eddie Madril in fancy dance regalia. Photo by Eva Kolenko, courtesy of Eva Kolenko.   46

Figure 2.7. Student Kouncil of Intertribal Nations (SKINS), 2012 pow-wow flyer. Designed by Ashley Richards, courtesy of SKINS. 54

Figure 3.1. Construction of Native American vertical whistle flute. Reproduced from *The Art of the Native American Flute*, 1996, Canyon Records. Courtesy of Canyon Records. 58

Figure 3.2. Doc Tate Nevaquaya, 1978, Oklahoma City, Oklahoma. Photo by Verna Gillis, courtesy of Verna Gillis. 63

Figure 3.3. R. Carlos Nakai, *c.*1997. Photo by John Running, courtesy of Canyon Records. 69

Figure 4.1. Buffy Sainte-Marie, Down East Music Festival, Homer, Alaska, 2012. Photo by Heidi Aklaseaq Senungetuk, courtesy of Heidi Aklaseaq Senungetuk. 83

Figure 4.2. (Left to right) John-Carlos Perea, Floyd Red Crow Westerman, and Jacob Perea, Native Contemporary Arts Festival, San Francisco, *c.*1995. Photo by Barbara Perea, courtesy of the author. 85

Figure 4.3. XIT, *c.*1973. (Back row, left to right) Obie Sullivan, Leeja Herrera, Jomac Suazo, R. C. Gariss Jr. (Front row, left to right) Chili Yazzie, Tom Bee, Tyrone King. Photo by Alton Walpole, courtesy of Tom Bee, SOAR Records, © 1973 Tom Bee. All rights reserved. 89

Figure 5.1. Oscar Pettiford, *The New Oscar Pettiford Sextet*, 1999. Courtesy of Concord Music Group. 101

Figure 5.2. Ron Thorne (drums), Jim Pepper (saxophone), "Spirit Days," June 19, 1987, Anchorage, Alaska. Photo by Patti Thorne, from the collection of Ron and Patti Thorne. 103

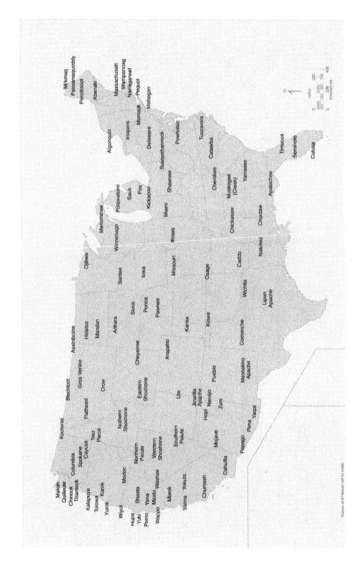

MAP P.1 *Map of tribal areas in the United States* *(designed by Monica Magtoto, magtotoart.com).*

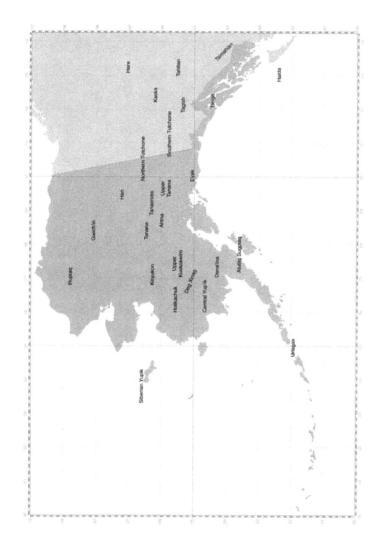

MAP P.2 *Map of tribal areas in Alaska* *(designed by Monica Magtoto, magtotoart.com).*

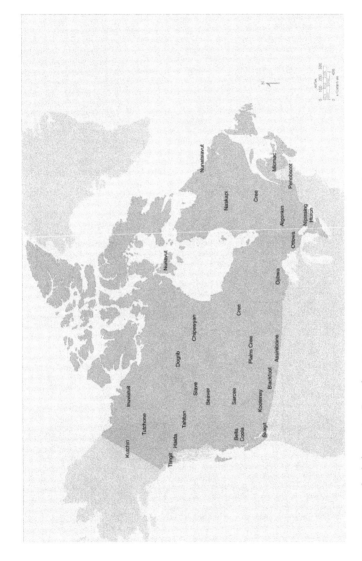

MAP P.3 *Map of tribal areas in Canada* *(designed by Monica Magtoto, magtotoart.com).*

.

Timeline of Songs and Events Referenced in the Text

June 25, 1876	Battle of Little Bighorn
1879–1918	Carlisle Indian Industrial School
1883–1910	Buffalo Bill's Wild West show
December 29, 1890	Wounded Knee Massacre
1937–1938	Mildred Bailey, "Rockin' Chair"
1939–1945	World War II
1941	Belo Cozad, "Kiowa Story of the Flute"
1950–1960	Federal Relocation Program
1951	Canyon Records founded
1956	Oscar Pettiford, "Stardust"
1963	Peter La Farge, "Custer"
1964	Buffy Sainte-Marie, "Now that the Buffalo's Gone"
1964	Louis Armstrong and his All-Stars with Russell Moore, "I Still Get Jealous"
1966	Indian House Records founded
November 20, 1969 to June 11, 1971	Occupation of Alcatraz Island by Indians of All Tribes
1971	XIT, "End?"
1975	Kiowa Dance Group Singers, "Kiowa Flag Song"
1978	Ironwood Singers, "Round Dance" and "Little Bighorn Victory Song"
1978	"Courting Song," Tom Mauchahty-Ware.
1978	Porcupine Singers, "Lakota National Anthem (Flag Song) and Veterans' Song"
1979	Doc Tate Nevaquaya, "Flute Wind Song Intro" and "Flute Wind Song"
1983	Kevin Locke, "The Photograph"
1986	Silver Wave Records founded

1987	R. Carlos Nakai, "Shaman's Call"
1988	Jim Pepper, "Witchi Tia To"
1989	Sound of America Records founded
1991	Jim Pepper, "Witchi Tai To"
1996	Black Lodge Singers, "Straight Intertribal"
1997	R. Carlos Nakai, James DeMars, and the Canyon Symphony Orchestra, "Two World Concerto: Lake That Speaks"
2000	Northern Cree, "Home of the Warriors"
2001	Best Native American Album Grammy category and award inaugurated
2001	Young Bird, "Road Warrior"
2002	Mary Youngblood, "Beneath the Raven Moon"
2006	Elk Soldier, "Hoka Hey"
2011	Best Native American Album Grammy category restructured, becomes part of new Regional Roots category
2012	Northern Cree, "Facebook Drama"

CHAPTER 1

Thinking about Intertribal Native American Music

What is **Native American** music? What does it mean to "sound" Native American? If you are a filmgoer, you may hear "the sound of Indian" (Deloria 2004, 183–223) in the drum **beat** and melodies of early Western film soundtracks. Other film aficionados might hear the sound of Indian in the accents and speech patterns of Victor Joseph and Thomas Builds-The-Fire in Chris Eyre's (Cheyenne and Arapaho) *Smoke Signals* (2001). For many sports fans the performance of the Atlanta Braves' "Tomahawk Chop" and countless other school fight songs sound their own variant of Native American sonic identity. If you are a reader you may hear Indian sounds through the voices of Indian authors such as Simon Ortiz (Acoma Pueblo), Joy Harjo (Mvskoke [Creek]), and Sherwin Bitsui (Diné [Navajo]). Or, you may associate the sound of Indian with Native musicians in **genres** ranging from **pow-wow** and Native American flute music to rock, jazz, classical, and beyond. This is all to say that the "sound" of Native Americans and of Native American musics is as potentially diverse in source and style—and as audible—as those of any other culture at the present moment.

> **ACTIVITY 1.1** *Are you familiar with the names and genres I mentioned in the previous paragraph? If not, search the Internet to familiarize yourself with the names and sounds through web pages and video if available. In relation to Western films it may be helpful to specify a director's name, such as John Ford.*

Beverley Diamond's *Native American Music in Eastern North America*, the first volume on that topic in the Global Music Series, examines Native

American musics and musicians with the aim of "explor[ing] contrasting expectations about Native American sound and song, focusing on the northern and eastern regions of North America" (Diamond 2008, 2). This textbook continues the work begun in Diamond's volume by introducing various **intertribal** genres of historical and contemporary Native American music and the musicians that perform them, making audible the diversity and complexity of musical expressions produced by Native American artists. While Diamond chose to structure her explorations around the geographic markers of northern and eastern North America, I have chosen to expand upon her approach and focus instead upon *intertribal* Native American musics in the United States. While there are many genres of Native American music that could be classified as intertribal, I will focus on those genres in which I participate as both an ethnomusicologist and as a performer: pow-wow singing, Native American flute, and popular musics such as folk, rock, and jazz.

The decision to focus the scope of this textbook in this fashion is not simply a practical one; participation as viewed through attention to fieldwork, performance, or other means is a hallmark of ethnomusicology as a discipline. This book proceeds from an understanding that knowledge about intertribal Native American music is constructed and negotiated not only through observation and analysis but also through participation. My participation in the above-mentioned genres then provides a window through which to observe, analyze, and facilitate discussion with you, the reader, on a variety of topics over the course of this work. You will also participate in the creation and negotiation of knowledge about intertribal Native American music in the United States by reading the text, listening to the musical examples on the accompanying compact disc and online, and engaging in discussions facilitated by the activities in the following chapters and influenced by your own lived experiences. By foregrounding participation in this way I intend to problematize the notion of an oppositional relationship between self and other or the observer and the observed. Rather than simply learn about "others" in the course of reading, you will also have the opportunity to discuss how you relate or do not relate to the subject and issues at hand.

This textbook and the songs on the accompanying compact disc and Ping playlist are intended to make audible the many different ways in which it is possible to "sound Native American." I challenge the expectation that Native American cultures are static and exist "authentically" only in their past histories. The musicians you will experience in the course of reading this book are important because of the way their **musicking** takes place in and is relevant to the present moment.

This is not to say that a connection to and respect for the past are not important; it is, however, to recognize that a connection to the past must serve the needs of Native American musicians and their communities in the present moment as they work toward a shared future.

Given my focus on a selected set of genres, it should also be noted that the sounds covered here are not the "only" musical means through which Native Americans construct their identities. While my life experiences may sound like pow-wow music and jazz, those of others may sound like the country music of Buddy Red Bow (Oglala Lakota), the punk rock of Blackfire (Diné [Navajo]), or the hip hop of War Party (Hobbema Cree). The fact that those and other musicians are not discussed in this text is made less problematic by the fact that the genres, concepts, and questions discussed here are offered not as the "final word" on intertribal Native American music in the United States. Instead, using my lived experiences as a guide and recognizing the diversity of **Indigenous** experiences, I want this work to serve as part of a larger discussion about the many genres that comprise intertribal Native American music and about the ways in which it can be taught in different contexts.

It is my hope that you will take the opportunity as you read through this text to question and to challenge your own expectations of Native Americans and Native American music. That process, in my way of thinking, does not involve the accumulation of definitive answers as much as it involves the willingness to ask questions, to think about the answers, and to continue the process of questioning. Following the example of Bonnie C. Wade's introductory volume in the Global Music Series *Thinking Musically* (2009), I will begin in this chapter by asking you to think about a number of different concepts relevant to how you and I perceive and understand the process of music making. To that end, I have structured the book around the framework of **soundings**, a concept that provides one way to think about music and, more importantly, about what people "do" when they perform, listen to, or otherwise take part in the process of making music.

I am also going to ask you to think about time. When I say "time" in the context of a music class you may think of discussing **rhythm**, **speed**, and their organization in a particular song. While you would be correct, and I will point out those aspects as you progress through the text, I also want to expand your thinking about time to include linear versus **circular time**. These concepts will be helpful to thinking about Native Americans and Native American music as not existing solely in the past but as sounding in the past, present, and future.

After thinking about soundings and time, I will focus in on the concept of intertribalism as a modifier for the genres of music to be addressed in this volume. What does intertribal mean and how is it relevant to the study of Native American music? That question points to the need to think about the names given to the people who are the subject of this study. I will close this chapter and transition to the next by introducing myself to you and explaining the importance of an introduction in the context of a pow-wow.

THINKING ABOUT SOUNDINGS

In my **American Indian** music classes, I like to begin by asking students to define "music." This question can have different meanings depending on your cultural references, life experiences, and any number of other factors. The melodic recitation of the Qur'an, while music to non-Muslim ears, "is not considered *musiqa* . . . a category encompassing genres (that is, types of music) that may elicit negative associations of secular musical practice," as opposed to spiritual life (Wade 2009, 7). I appreciate this example of contrasting attitudes toward what constitutes music because it points to the fact that music is not simply a thing. Following the example of musicologist Christopher Small (1998), I encourage you to think of music not as a static thing or an object but as a social activity. By thinking of music as an activity, I invite you to consider that the act of listening is as essential to the production and reception of music as is the act of performing it. Each of us becomes a musician in this way regardless of whether or not we play an instrument.

In keeping with this focus on music as a social activity, throughout this text I will refer to pow-wow soundings, cedar flute soundings, Native folk, rock, and jazz soundings. When I use the term "soundings," I am trying to indicate that the musicians you are learning about and the recordings you are listening to are not simply things or products. They represent the collective activity of a group of individuals that includes the musicians, their families, friends, and listeners. In addition, the recordings included on the accompanying compact disc and online represent the collective activity of producers and corporate interests—in essence anyone involved with the creation of that musical moment. Time must also be taken into account in terms of thinking about individuals from the past who made it possible for these musical moments to exist in the present and those whom these musical moments may or may not influence in the future.

In light of this simultaneous complexity, the concept of soundings is helpful because it recognizes the individual and communal aspects of music making and destabilizes the idea that music is a thing or object. That attention to the social activity of music making will be foregrounded in the following chapters. For example, as you proceed to the chapter on pow-wow music (chapter 2), I will discuss the communal influence of large-scale intertribalism on pow-wow practice and I will point out the moments where specific individual tribal practices inform pow-wow music making. In the case of cedar flute music, I will discuss the ways in which tribal-specific flute repertoires combine with Western musical **tunings** and influences to create the complex sound of cedar flute as heard in contemporary practice. It is in the balance between individual and communal agency that the fluid, complex beauty of intertribal Native American music becomes audible.

The concept of soundings is also useful in that it allows me to point out the various types of work that people use music to accomplish in their lives. A recording on its own does nothing. Whether you and I speak of a record, compact disc, or mp3, in each case one of us must put the needle down, press, or click "play" in order to hear the music. Your decision to press "play" is very important as you are enabling music to be heard and in doing so that musical moment can travel from one listener to another. Everyone presses "play" or—to extend the analogy—attends live performances of their favorite music, or seeks out new music for unique and individual reasons. Those reasons are important because they speak to the way individuals use music in their everyday lives. Rather than make reference to what I perceive to be the inanimate nature of the term "recording," the use of "soundings" also helps illuminate the many uses to which music is put by listeners and the fluidity of those uses over time. This will facilitate discussion of the sounding of communities through pow-wow music in chapter 2, the sounding of revitalization through cedar flute music in chapter 3, the sounding of alliances and activism through Native American popular music during the 1960s and early 1970s in chapter 4, and—drawing upon the work of cultural historian Philip Deloria (Dakota)—the sounding of "expectation," "anomaly," and "unexpectedness" (Deloria 2004, 3–15) through Native jazz musicians in chapter 5.

To review, I will use the term "soundings" as a guiding concept throughout the rest of the text to refer to the individual and communal experiences informing the ways in which intertribal Native American music in the United States is performed and heard by musicians and listeners. I will also apply the term to make audible the various forms of work accomplished when Native American musicians perform their music in different genres and performance contexts.

THINKING ABOUT TIME: PAST, PRESENT, AND FUTURE

As musicians—and here I am speaking of anyone who participates in the activity of making music either by performing or listening—time can have any number of culturally and contextually specific meanings. In my experience as a pow-wow singer and cedar flute player, I have found that time has just as much to do with a sense of one's personal history making music as it does with an understanding of **pulse** or **tempo**. In this section I will elaborate on an explanation of time passed on to me by Florinda Gushoney and her son Orlando Gushoney (both White Mountain Apache). I am grateful to them for their guidance, generosity, and support in sharing this way of thinking with me.

Many of us are raised with a linear conception of time, in which time may be thought of as a chain of distinct events—past, present, and future, as seen in Figure 1.1.

While this is a perfectly reasonable way to think of time, it can have the effect of limiting the potential for thinking about the ways past, present, and future relate to each other. In a linear concept of time, the past is that which has already happened, the present is happening "now," and the future is that which has yet to happen.

In order to emphasize the interrelationship between past, present, and future time, I would like to encourage you to think in terms of circular time as illustrated in Figure 1.2.

Circular time finds past, present, and future taking place simultaneously. While this may seem strange at first, I would argue that it is not so different from ways of thinking you might already be used to. To share a personal example, my maternal grandmother passed away while I was in the process of writing this textbook. In linear terms, it would be common to think of her as no longer being "here" and therefore as having

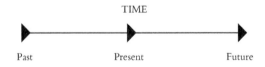

FIGURE 1.1 *Visual representation of linear time* (designed by Monica Magtoto, magtotoart.com).

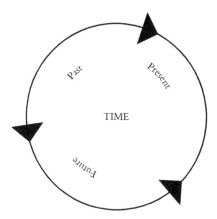

FIGURE 1.2 *Visual representation of circular time* *(designed by Monica Magtoto, magtotoart.com).*

lived in my "past." Circular time, on the other hand, reminds us that the past and present are simultaneous and interactive. My family and I tell stories about my grandmother every day. We have objects that belonged to her that we now carry as a way of remembering her. When we remember my grandmother my family and I bring the past into the present moment. When I tell stories about my grandmother to my daughter, I take the presentness of my grandmother and extend that to make my grandmother part of my daughter's future, illustrating the interaction between past and present as well as past, present, and future time.

ACTIVITY 1.2 *My example of the way I think about my grandmother's passing helps to illustrate circular time by showing how my past is also part of my present and future. Another personal example of circular time is my own name: John-Carlos. I am named for my maternal and paternal grandfathers. By keeping those names in our family we keep those memories of the past relevant in the present and future. Make a list of examples relevant to your own life that illustrate circular time by showing how your past is also part of your present and your future. You can also expand the exercise by thinking about how your present relates to your past and future or how your future plans are related to your present and past.*

This attention to different cultural concepts of time applies Indigenous frameworks to the study of music in culture. When I think of lessons learned from engaging with a circular concept of time, I think first of learning a sense of responsibility. In each case, when I think of the relationship between past, present, and future I am confronted with the responsibility of what it means to be a Native musician and to speak and teach about Native musics. It is by no means stretching the imagination or historical narrative to say that in the past women, men, and children have in some cases sacrificed their lives in order to make sure some of the musics addressed in this text remain audible in the world. This is, however, no different from any other culture's music. Regardless of where we come from, we have a responsibility to the people whose sacrifices carried us into this present and have implications for all our futures.

This book then provides an opportunity for readers to think about and to discuss different issues relating to the activity of music. The conversations we have in the present must take into account our individual and collective pasts as well as the needs of our present and our future. The interactions that occur through this book and through the conversations it will hopefully motivate will have effects in the future that none of us can foresee. So, paraphrasing artist Jimmie Durham (Cherokee) (1993, 147), it is necessary that we all speak well and listen well out of respect for where we have come from (the past), where we are (the present), and where we are going (the future). In this way you can begin to see that thinking about time in relation to Native American music in this textbook will involve musical matters as well as philosophical ones intended to deepen your understanding and experience of the musics discussed here.

THINKING ABOUT INTERTRIBALISM

By calling this textbook *Intertribal Native American Music in the United States*, I want to draw attention to the fact that while every tribe has songs and dances that are used for specific functions and in specific contexts, an interactive culture of intertribal exchange has simultaneously been inspiring new musical and artistic forms over time. Given contemporary histories of Native relocation, many Native people do not have immediate access to their tribal-specific ways of being. Intertribal culture provides a point of access for those individuals to experience and construct their identities on a macro level through social inter-action and in doing so to better understand the particularity of their tribal specificity. For some who do not have access to tribal specific-ity, the intertribal space can even become a primary identity. Given the importance of thinking about intertribalism to Native music studies I am interested in making these intertribal musical cultures audible in public and academic discourses in order to expand the available schol-arship and to deepen the conversation on what it means to be Native and intertribal.

To say that something is intertribal means that it takes into account a coming together of many different tribal lifeways and viewpoints. In this way "intertribal" may be thought of not only as a general geo-graphic distinction referring to social, political, or economic engage-ments between different groups, but also as a cultural distinction. An intertribal pow-wow, for example, is a pow-wow that is not run accord-ing to the practices of a single tribe. Instead it takes its direction from the constantly renegotiated practices of many different tribes. An intertribal dance at a pow-wow may draw together into the arena dancers from all parts of the country representing different men's and women's dance categories to dance socially. Depending on the interaction between the **pow-wow committee** and the **Master of Ceremonies**, the dance might also involve participation from Native and non-Native spectators. Intertribal dancing thus becomes a moment during a pow-wow where difference is negotiated and community is created through social activ-ity of music and dance.

My use of the term "intertribal" responds to contemporary discus-sions on the use of **pan-Indian** and "intertribal" in scholarly work on American Indians. Many definitions of the term "pan-Indianism" have been discussed and contested over time by scholars in ethnomusicol-ogy, anthropology, and American Indian Studies (for example, Howard 1955; Young 1981; Fixico 2000; Lobo and Peters 2001; Lobo et al. 2002, Perea 2009). James Howard is credited as a primary ethnomusico-logical source in the establishment and use of the term "pan-Indian," but given that his definition highlighted loss—"the process by which sociocultural entities . . . are *losing* their tribal distinctiveness and in its place are developing a nontribal 'Indian' culture" (1955, 215, my emphasis)—I find that "pan-Indian" can sometimes carry an implicit negative valuation.

Given the controversy over historical and contemporary usage of "pan-Indian," Clyde Ellis and Luke Lassiter suggested substituting "intertribal" for "pan-Indian," "a term widely preferred by participants themselves, and one that we believe more accurately describes both the common and negotiated ground of powwow culture" (2005, xiii). While my own background in pow-wow music leads me to favor the use of "intertribal" over "pan-Indian" as a descriptor, readers will encounter both terms in the course of studying American Indian musics and therefore I will alternate between "pan-Indian(ism)" and "intertribal(ism)" for the remainder of the textbook.

THINKING ABOUT NAMES AND TERMINOLOGY

ACTIVITY 1.3 *What words do you associate as similar or related to "American Indian?" Write them down, being sure to include both positive and negative associations.*

Many students will mention "Native American" as related to "American Indian," raising the question of which term is more proper in conversation. This is a difficult question to answer because of my own personal experience with "American Indian" and "Native American." Growing up in the San Francisco Bay Area, I was constantly aware of and affected by the historical influence of the occupation of Alcatraz Island by Indians of All Tribes on November 20, 1969, and so the term "Indian" has a great deal of political significance for me. On the other hand, I also remember a personal experience that took place during a visit to San Francisco in the mid-1990s by my aunt and uncle from Dulce, New Mexico. We took a boat tour of Alcatraz and, as we circled the island, I noticed my aunt looking at the large sign proclaiming Alcatraz's status as "INDIAN LAND." My aunt turned to me, shrugged in the direction of the sign, and said quietly "I'm not Indian . . . I'm Apache." This experience taught me that while the Alcatraz occupation may have politicized the terms "American Indian" and "Indian," those same events were not received and interpreted the same way by all Native people.

While I tend to use "American Indian" more than "Native American" in conversation, and while the terms are to a degree interchangeable, it is equally important that attention be paid to specific tribal affiliation(s). "Native American," "American Indian," and "Indian" are useful descriptors but they are also generalizations; there are more than five hundred Native nations currently recognized by the United States federal government and more than two hundred that are seeking federal recognition. This diversity cannot and should not be oversimplified through the use of general naming terminology. While I may refer interchangeably to "Native Americans," "American Indians," and "Indians" throughout this text, I will also specify wherever possible an individual's tribal affiliations in parentheses following their name; in my case, it would look like this: John-Carlos Perea (Mescalero Apache, Irish, German, Chicano). In this way the reader will have a balanced understanding of both general and more specific naming practices. Keep in mind that an individual's tribal affiliation should not be understood as communicating a single, static set of traits or behaviors. As I illustrate in the chapter on pow-wow music, part of the importance of intertribal Native American music in the United States lies in the ability of its artists and audiences to negotiate complex differences in order to make music and culture meaningful.

ACTIVITY 1.4 *Familiarize yourself with the tribal names provided on the maps of the lower forty-eight United States, Alaska, and Canada in Maps 1–3. Were you aware of the tribes living in these areas?*

Other terms that often come up in an introductory discussion of naming are **First Nations** and **Alaska Native**. "First Nations" refers to one of the three Indigenous groups recognized by the Canadian Constitution of 1982, the other two being Inuit and Métis (Diamond 2008, 4). In that light I use First Nations only where relevant to the Indigenous inhabitants of Canada, although recent publications in American Indian ethnomusicology do make the case for wider application and usage (see Browner 2009). This recognition of First Nations as a distinction is especially important in the context of the present work. Although the title of this textbook specifies a focus on the United States, the interaction between Native nations in the United States and Canada has greatly shaped intertribal Native American music culture, as can be seen, for example, in the influence of Cree pow-wow **drum** group Northern Cree on pow-wow singing in the United States. This influence speaks to shared traditions of Native mobility and cosmopolitanism and will be highlighted where appropriate in the following chapters.

The culture of intertribal exchange between Native nations in the United States and Canada, as well as between tribal nations within the United States, is important to recognize for the way in which those exchanges cross boundaries between states and countries and in doing so call those boundaries into question. As in the previously cited example of Northern Cree, one can argue that the sound of pow-wow music in the United States is as much a First Nations production as it is American Indian. Buffy Sainte-Marie is another highly visible public figure, whose career moves back and forth across the political boundary separating the United States and Canada and in doing so makes that boundary more permeable when it is listened to rather that seen. In this way the activist potential of intertribal Native American music can be heard not simply as an articulation of American identity but also as a factor in the construction of an Indigenous identity.

The term Alaska Native, as employed by the Alaska Federation of Natives, refers to Inuit (Eskimo), Indians, and Aleuts. In the same way that my Jicarilla Apache aunt did not necessarily identify as Indian, Alaska Natives do not necessarily identify as American Indians. Although American Indians and Alaska Natives are combined together on census forms and other documentation, individuals from both groups lead lives informed by unique historical and contemporary circumstances. Consider, for example, that when discussing histories of colonization many Alaska Natives speak not of Christopher Columbus but of Vitus Bering and James Cook. Please be attentive to these distinctions as they appear throughout this textbook and your own studies of Native musics.

When I discuss naming with students in my classes they will also bring up more uncomfortable words such as "redskin," "brave," "savage," and "squaw." I think it is incredibly important that these words are voiced and brought out into the open so they can be discussed and disempowered in the classroom context. While most often referred to as stereotypes, I follow Diamond's use of Deloria in her Global Music Series volume and qualify these descriptors, and others like them, as "expectations" of American Indians (Diamond 2008, 1–2; Deloria 2004, 3–15). In the same way that it is important to combat stereotypes, regardless of culture, gender, or any other identifier, it is also important to ask students to confront their expectations of American Indians. By engaging with your expectations of American Indians, or any culture whose music you study, you open yourself to a deeper and hopefully more meaningful learning experience because you learn about yourself and where you have come from as much as you learn about someone else.

ACTIVITY 1.5   *Make a list of your expectations of intertribal American Indian music. After you complete each book chapter, return to your list of expectations and keep track of which have changed and which have been confirmed.*

INTRODUCING MYSELF:
WHERE ARE YOU FROM?

It is common when attending pow-wows or other Native American gatherings to be asked, "Where are you from?" While the question may seem simple on the surface, I have found in my experience that it is asked to do much more than just locate a person. This type of question, and the information solicited by it, has cultural and academic significance in the context of Native music studies.

One of the foundational tenets of American Indian/Native American Studies is the centrality of land to Native identity formation. While recognizing the importance of this concept it should not be essentialized in a binary opposition that pits reservations and other "traditional" homelands against cities and urban centers. Native American studies scholar Jack Forbes (Powhatan, Delaware, 1934–2011) showed how a reinterpretation of the cultural expectations framing the definition of "urban" illuminates histories of urban **indigeneity** (Sissons 2005, 61–82) that date back to, for example, mound-building civilizations in the United States (Forbes 2001). When applied to the idea that land is central to Native American identity formation, Forbes's work points out that a sense of "land" in the present day, taking histories of colonization and relocation into account, cannot rely on static notions of where and what land is but instead must take the variation and fluidity of individual experience and mobility into account. In this way of thinking about place and identity, the idea of land is expanded beyond static governmentalized impositions to account for urbanization and movement in a way that emphasizes presence over absence (Perea 2011).

If the academic significance of "where are you from?" points to an expanded sense of land and the other spaces within which identity is formed, the question carries a similar intertribal cultural significance in the context of events such as pow-wows. When I am asked where I am from at a pow-wow, I understand it as a moment to discuss not just where I was born but the experiences through which I learned to sing and develop my musical practice. In the process, personal and musical histories are mapped on to the aforementioned historical narratives, and individuals situate themselves and their identities over time.

"Where are you from?" is, in this way of thinking, essential to understanding both intertribal Native American music in the United States and the way you, the reader and listener, relate to that music. Remember that music is not a thing, it is a social activity. It is important, then, in the context of the conversation facilitated by this textbook for you to understand where I come from and also for you to think about where you come from as part of your studies.

ACTIVITY 1.6 *Introduce yourself to your classmates using the following prompt: If you were trapped on a desert island and could have only four songs with you, what songs could you not live without? Describe why each song is important to you and your sense of personal identity. Be sure to provide the name of the performer, to describe the genre or type of music each performer is associated with in public, and to give a link to a performer website or social media webpage so your classmates can learn more about your desert island musicians on their own time.*

I was born in Dulce, New Mexico. My father is Mescalero Apache and Chicano from Las Cruces, New Mexico, and my mother is German and Irish from Long Island, New York. Not long after I was born, my parents moved from Dulce to San Francisco, California where I have spent most of my life. While I identify with and respect all of my different cultural heritages, I identify primarily as an urban Mescalero Apache.

Some of my earliest childhood memories involve my parents taking me to pow-wows in the San Francisco Bay Area. I do not want to give the impression, however, that I grew up listening only to pow-wow drums and cedar flutes as a child. Far from it, my family has eclectic musical tastes ranging from the Beatles and *musica tejana* to jazz, Irish, and classical music. It was not until I went to college at San Francisco State University that I began studying and singing with Dr. Bernard Hoehner, D.V.M. (Hunkpapa, Sihásapa), who, among many other things, was a **Northern Plains** pow-wow singer, Northern traditional dancer, pow-wow emcee, and lecturer in American Indian Studies at SFSU (see Figure 1.3).

FIGURE 1.3 *Dr. Bernard Hoehner at Three Rivers Pow-Wow, c. 1980s.* *Photo courtesy of the Hoehner family.*

Dr. Hoehner invited me to his pow-wow drum, and those experiences form the core of my knowledge about the contemporary intertribal pow-wow and the role of pow-wow music as a sonic marker of community, subjects to which I now turn in chapter 2.

Sounding Communities: Intertribal Pow-wow Music

Some of my earliest pow-wow memories involve attending the San Francisco State University (SFSU) pow-wow with my mother and father. At that time, the pow-wow was held on the basement level of the campus student center. The basement level was essentially a large room with food concessions against one wall and a video arcade against the other. During the day, food vendors sold pizza, Chinese food, and sandwiches to students who either took their food to go or sat and ate at the tables positioned throughout the space. Students could also sit in a balcony area overlooking the basement floor.

As a child I was already familiar with the basement of the campus student center from time spent there with my father. He began his career as a teacher and administrator at SFSU soon after I was born, and I would spend afternoons there with him while he was working. I was used to seeing the space full of students eating and coming and going. Of the day I went to my first pow-wow, my memory is not of students but of the sound of the drum. It was something I remember both hearing and feeling as we walked into the student center. On that day the pizza and Chinese food vendors were closed and a fry bread stand was open in its place selling Indian tacos, circular pieces of puffy, fried bread topped with meat, cheese, onions, tomato, and hot sauce, plain fry bread to be topped with honey or powdered sugar, coffee, and soft drinks. As we walked downstairs toward the pow-wow we passed other vendors selling everything from jewelry and other handcrafted pieces of artwork to audiocassettes and tee shirts. At those vendor stands one could see spectators in street clothes standing next to pow-wow dancers dressed in full dance regalia doing their shopping, eating their food, and talking to one another. By the time my father and I reached the balcony level and looked over the basement, the sound of the drum made speaking to my parents impossible. We stood and watched and listened to the pow-wow.

When I think back to standing there looking out over my first pow-wow with my father, my clearest memories are those involving the sounds of the pow-wow. I remember hearing the higher **pitch** singing of Northern Plains pow-wow singers (CD tracks 1, 2, 4, 6, 7, 8, 9) and the lower pitch singing of **Southern Plains** pow-wow singers (CD tracks 3, 5) and feeling small in the face of their power. I remember hearing the sound of dancer's bells keeping time with the beat of the drum as they moved in a circle around the pow-wow arena. I remember the sound of the master of ceremonies speaking over the public address system explaining the dance to spectators and encouraging dancers to dance harder. And, throughout everything, the pulse of the pow-wow drum propelling the dancers, spectators, and event forward.

Regardless of where you live in the United States the chances are very good that at some point during the year a pow-wow will take place in a community near you. In my classes at SFSU I begin discussions

FIGURE 2.1 *Northern Cree Singers, Saddle Lake Pow-Wow, Saddle Lake First Nation, Alberta, Canada, 2011.* Photo by Stephen Butler, courtesy of Canyon Records.

of pow-wow with the following definition: Pow-wows are intertribal Native American social gatherings built around a shared repertoire of songs and dances. That definition, however, is not comprehensive and provides only an initial foundation through which to understand the complexity of pow-wows in the present day. For example, the social nature of pow-wow culture is counterbalanced by a spiritual component articulated by many singers, dancers, and spectators. That sense of spirituality cannot be generalized as it is unique to the tribal and intertribal backgrounds and lived experiences of each individual. The relationship between individual tribal-specific practices and intertribal sharing relating to music, dance, arts, crafts, and lifeways means that as Native communities grow and change so too will pow-wows change every time they are held.

Pow-wows have become interactive spaces for Native and non-Native communities to educate each other and, as a consequence, to create new forms of culture relevant to the needs of the people who attend pow-wows. This means that there are potentially as many different ways to pow-wow as there are tribes in the United States. Even individuals who identify with the same Native nation may pow-wow differently for their own unique reasons. If you were to ask someone else to introduce the pow-wow to you, the chances are very good you would get a completely different set of explanations from the ones provided here. In my experience, this is why pow-wows continue to remain relevant: they provide space for the creation and negotiation of culture through intertribal music and dance for successive generations of participants.

POW-WOW ORIGIN STORIES

As educator Gregory Cajete (Tewa) explains, "Native peoples have particular understandings of the way the world has come into being, and the ways they have come into being as people" (Cajete 2000, 31). This accumulated knowledge is conveyed through *origin story*—"recount[ing] the migration of the people through the landscape with stops where important lessons about relationships, ideals, and moral teachings must be learned" (33). In keeping with my explanation of circular time, you might think of origin stories as narratives that explain where people came from in the past, how they have come to be in the present moment, and what their future might be. There are many different types of origin stories, ranging from tribal-specific Native American stories to the story of Adam and Eve and beyond. I am applying the concept and using it in this case in order to explain to you my own sense of where pow-wow comes from, how it has come to be in the present moment, and the ways in which it may change in the future.

> **ACTIVITY 2.1** *What is your origin story? Where did you come from? Where are your parents from? Write out your origin story in bullet points and tell it to a classmate. Does your sense of origin involve your religious belief? Discuss with your classmates as far as it is comfortable and appropriate to your belief.*

By invoking the concept of origin story in the singular, I do not mean to imply that pow-wows emanate from a singular historical narrative. As ethnomusicologist Tara Browner (Choctaw) notes, "pow-wow origins are a contested topic in Indian circles" (Browner 2002, 19), and therefore while origin story offers a means through which to examine pow-wows in past, present, and future time, one pow-wow origin story cannot be mapped onto all Native pow-wow participants. Origin story is best understood as striking a balance, similar to that seen in pow-wows, between individual and/or tribal specificity and intertribal exchange. That is why I take the position that I must first speak from the basis of my participation in the genres discussed here, because that participation locates my relationship to other pow-wow narratives. In this way of thinking, the point of discussing pow-wow origin story is not a question of "firsts" but rather of attempting to understand how tribal-specific perspectives have influenced larger circuits of intertribal exchange.

My sense of pow-wow origin story is shaped through my participation in the event as a singer and spectator, as well as by readings on pow-wows drawn from ethnomusicology and Native American Studies. I was mentored in these areas by Dr. Bernard Hoehner, a Northern Plains singer, Northern traditional dancer, and pow-wow emcee. The perspectives he imparted to me can be qualified in pow-wow parlance as Northern Plains **style**.

Northern Plains is a geographic distinction used in pow-wow practice to denote music, dance, and other cultural influences emerging from tribes in the Northern Plains of the continental United States and up into Canada. Northern Plains style is contrasted with Southern Plains style, referring to music, dance, and other cultural influences emerging from tribes in the Southern Plains of the United States. It should be noted that Northern Plains and Southern Plains are large-scale generalizations and within those generalizations one can find a tremendous amount of variation. For example, I qualify my experiences as Northern Plains because of my interaction with Dr. Hoehner but, geographically speaking, my home nation comes from the southwestern United States. So, keep in mind that these terms, like those discussed in relation to naming in chapter 1, must be understood as fluid and open to change.

Keeping in mind the immense influence of these geographic distinctions on intertribal pow-wow culture, I will synthesize my sense of Northern Plains pow-wow origin story with literature on Southern and Northern Plains pow-wows. The following overview draws upon sources from ethnomusicology, ethnography, anthropology, and Native studies. Given the depth of existing scholarship, readers are encouraged to use the following as a starting point and to investigate specific case studies to refine and expand their personal knowledge (for example, see Vennum 1982; Powers 1990; Young Bear and Theisz 1994; Lassiter 1998; Browner 2002; Ellis 2003; Ellis, Lassiter, and Dunham 2005).

The precursors to contemporary pow-wow dancing can be found in tribal military, dance, and other ceremonial societies unique to every tribe. Those society songs and dances, reflecting Indigenous worldviews on themes ranging from birth, death, religion, warfare, agriculture, intertribal alliances, and other subjects, came to be viewed with greater suspicion by the United States federal government in the late 1800s. During this time period, historical events such as the **Wounded Knee massacre** came to symbolize the end of the so-called **Indian Wars**, further opening the western United States to expansion and development. Tribal music and dance repertoires, understood as performances of identity, stood as an impediment to that assimilationist policy and were therefore forcibly repressed by the US government in the form of dance bans instituted by the US federal government, bans that effected both Northern and Southern Plains tribes (Browner 2002, 28–9; Ellis 2003, 14–16).

In the face of genocide, forced assimilation, and relocation to reservations, Native Americans were left with limited options as to how they performed their music and dance. As individuals and tribes negotiated this complex historical moment many songs and dances began a process of transformation into what we now call "pow-wow." Dr. Hoehner taught that music and dance had to "go away" at this point in history in order to come back stronger and safer. One of the spaces Native

American music and dance "went" during this period was to become a form of entertainment for non-Native audiences.

Venues such as Buffalo Bill's Wild West were popular for performing the aforementioned struggle and eventual triumph of civilization over savagery. While the idea of Native men and women dancing as entertainment may be painful to consider, it is also important to recognize that the men and women who continued to dance in these venues went on to innovate both pow-wow dance styles and elements of pow-wow practice that are taken for granted in today's intertribal pow-wow culture. For example, Severt Young Bear (Oglala Lakota) noted that a pow-wow grand entry, where all of the assembled dancers dance into the arena for the first time, was as much influenced by warrior society parades as it was by Wild West shows and rodeo parades (Young Bear and Theisz 1994, 54). Historian Clyde Ellis points out that "increasingly faster and more exciting dancing" became popular for non-Native audiences and Native performers through the Wild West shows, laying the foundation for the development of contemporary fancy dancing (Ellis 2003, 112). Ellis also points out that these types of performance opportunities during the period of dance prohibition—from the 1880s until Bureau of Indian Affairs commissioner John Collier Sr. rescinded those bans in 1934—provided a means of economic opportunity for Native people, professionalizing Indian music and dance long before the advent of big-budget pow-wows and a commercial pow-wow music recording industry (2003, 79–101).

These musicians and dancers maintained community and created new communities through their efforts. Those communities were intertribal in makeup, drawing from tribes in both the Northern and Southern Plains of the United States and reflecting Native American relocation within the United States, forced and otherwise. By the 1920s, Natives began to take more control over the performance context, and the use of the term pow-wow became more prominent (Browner 2002, 30; Ellis 2003, 120–27). Although research has pinpointed various dates for the "first" intertribal pow-wow, Dr. Hoehner preferred to examine the origin story of the pow-wow as delineated by important events that helped shape the functional use of the event over time and I will continue following his example.

Following the legalization of Native American religious dance in the 1930s, pow-wows became prominent forums for the honoring of veterans during World War II. Families would sponsor a dance for a loved one entering the service and, on their return, they were welcomed home as a warrior with a dance. If the loved one did not return from service they remained part of the pow-wow community by being memorialized in songs and dances. Dr. Hoehner was a WWII veteran himself, so this moment in history played an important role in shaping the repertoire of songs he taught to me and to other students at SFSU. Many of the first pow-wow songs I learned are songs honoring veterans from WWII and from Vietnam. In this fashion one can see that the relationship of pow-wow dancing to warrior societies was not lost; it was transformed over time in ways that remain relevant to pow-wow participants.

This tradition of honoring military service can be problematic for many students in their first introduction to the pow-wow. How can American Indians serve in the military of the country that attempted to colonize them? The reasons Native American men and women choose to serve are as varied as the reasons people pow-wow, but I have found that a common theme among servicemen and women I have met is not allegiance to a particular political agenda but service to one's community. This type of thinking resituates the idea of what it means to be a soldier and adds new layers to the sense of community being sounded through pow-wow music and dance.

In the 1950s and 1960s, pow-wows became prominent as an urban community-organizing tool in part as a response to the Federal **Relocation** Program. Begun in the early 1950s, **Relocation** was a US government policy offering incentives to American Indians who chose to leave their reservation homes and relocate in various urban centers across the United States (Lobo and Peters 2001, ix). While Relocation was phrased in terms favorable to Native nations at the time of its implementation, contemporary historical analysis views Relocation as part of the US government's continued appropriation of American Indian lands (Fixico 2000, 4). That appropriation was to be accomplished by removing Indian people from their homelands, and from the communities present on those homelands, and in so doing to physically and mentally relocate American Indians to the modern urban environment.

I live in the San Francisco Bay Area, a major Indian Relocation center. Growing up, I met Indians who came from everywhere and, in many cases, whose families had come to the Bay Area as part of the Relocation program. While the purpose of that program may have been to break up American Indian communities, the reality was quite different. Friendship houses and community centers were formed by urban Natives to address the needs of local communities, including the Intertribal Friendship House in Oakland, California, and the

Friendship House Association of American Indians in San Francisco. These organizations saw Native people from different parts of the country, who might never have had the chance to meet, coming together to find support and community social interaction—and one of the many ways that community was fostered was through pow-wows. Pow-wows during this time period allowed for urban community building and the dissemination of different dances and songs in urban Native centers, and they also created a zone in which non-Indian spectators could begin to interact with and learn from these events.

In the 1960s and 1970s, the pow-wow took on a new sense of politicization in relation to the activities of the Red Power Movement, discussed in relation to the occupation of Alcatraz Island in chapter 4. I understand the Red Power Movement as an intertribal American Indian Civil Rights movement founded upon student activism, such as the National Indian Youth Council (Shreve 2011) and Indians of All Tribes (Johnson 2008), and occupations, such as the fish-ins in the Pacific Northwest and the occupation of Alcatraz Island (Johnson 2008). Pow-wow music and dance, and the communities who are formed around and through their performance, have always been political in nature, as can be seen from the aforementioned histories of the government dance bans. In the 1970s, that new politicization linked pow-wow music and culture with national events through actions like the creation of the American Indian Movement song (Young Bear and Theisz 1994, 155–7). While it was still a political act for Native people to sing and dance in resistance to historical legacies of repression and assimilation, those repertoires of music and dance were now linked to new currents of political activism and shared nationally by intertribal communities.

Whereas previous decades of pow-wow practice may be characterized by patterns of exchange, in my memory of the 1980s and 1990s a trend toward cultural specificity emerged. This is not to say the basis of the pow-wow changed, as an intertribal gathering founded upon an intertribal repertoire of songs and dance; it is to say that at this moment in time it became important to know and understand the component parts from which one's community was created. It is common at pow-wows to hear speakers begin an oration with the phrase: "Where I am from" in order to locate themselves and their position in relation to pow-wow practices, allowing listeners to develop a greater appreciation for the diversity of the pow-wow. Emcees and other speakers became more overt with references to tribal-specific practices, creating spaces at the pow-wow in which it was possible to relate in both intertribal and tribal-specific fashions. This corresponds to Browner's assertion that pow-wows "have a larger, underlying tribal or regional framework, and by either merging with or deviating from it participants reinforce personal tribal affiliations" (Browner 2002, 4). For example, when I grew up attending pow-wows in the San Francisco Bay Area I was exposed to Lakota pow-wow practices on the Northern Plains side and Kiowa pow-wow practices on the Southern Plains side. Exposure to those ways allowed me to learn about and to participate in intertribal exchange while also helping me define what it meant to be Mescalero Apache.

Over the past ten years of participating in pow-wows, I have found that innovations in technology, such as smart phones, have irrevocably changed the ways in which the event is experienced. Dr. Hoehner's introduction to pow-wow etiquette began with the admonition to "leave your camera at home," as it was, and to some degree still is, considered disrespectful to take pictures of dancers and singers without their consent. From his generational perspective, he felt that pow-wows should be experienced without technological distraction.

That kind of prohibition is almost impossible to monitor today, given the popularity of social networking websites and the fact that many of us carry still and video cameras in our pockets everywhere we go. Whereas I once attended pow-wows where drum and dance were recorded only with the permission of the lead or head singer and recordings were made onto audiocassette, it is not uncommon today to see pow-wow spectators, Native and non-Native, rush around drums groups with phones and tablets raised to capture a song or dance, which is then uploaded and made available to the world. The 2012 Gathering of Nations pow-wow in New Mexico, known for its large grand entry featuring thousands of dancers, featured a first-person online video broadcast from a camera attached to a dancer's head. So, while I still caution students about taking pictures and video at pow-wows, I also acknowledge that caution is generational on my part and future events will define the role of those technologies for coming generations.

During my experiences I have found that the subject of female pow-wow singers has played an equally influential role in the development of pow-wows. The subject of who sings or who dances is incredibly powerful, as it reflects interrelated issues of power and access to culture. Dr. Hoehner discussed these relationships through the example of the Four Circles, to which I will now turn.

> ACTIVITY 2.2 *Go to powwows.com and make a list of pow-wows in your area. If the pow-wows have websites with background historical information, review that information and see how it intersects with or diverges from the outline provided above.*

POW-WOW SPACE

If music is a social activity, then the social relationships that create the conditions of possibility for a pow-wow can be heard and, as I will show in this section, visualized as "sounding a community." To be sure, this community will take different forms relating to tribal and intertribal variations. In order to visualize the place and function of pow-wow music within the social context of a pow-wow gathering, Dr. Hoehner described a pow-wow as taking place within four circles. This type of metaphor has also been discussed in other studies of pow-wow music as way of understanding an individual's relationship to a larger whole (for example, see Young Bear and Theisz 1994, 177–9; Browner 2002, 98).

Dr. Hoehner's version of the four circles was passed on to me in the context of pow-wow drum rehearsal sessions as well as American Indian music classes at San Francisco State University. Before I continue, please remember that this concept is only one of many used to describe and to place pow-wow music. It is reflective of particular viewpoints that are in some cases tribally specific and in some cases individual to Dr. Hoehner's experience. Readers are encouraged to seek out other examples in order to develop the widest possible frame of reference reflective of the pow-wow as a diverse and complex event.

Dr. Hoehner explained that a pow-wow is made up of four circles, illustrated in Figure 2.2.

The pow-wow drum represents the first circle of the pow-wow. The drum is placed at the center of the pow-wow because its voice gathers singers, dancers, and other community members together to participate in the pow-wow. The drum is also placed at the center out of respect for the symbolism embedded in its construction (on drum construction, see Vennum 1982). It is constructed from elements representing the natural world within which human beings live. Drum frames may be made from different woods and drumheads are made from the hides

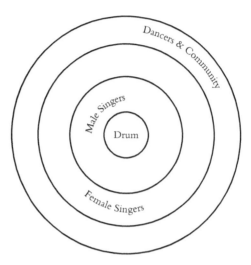

FIGURE 2.2 *Four circles of the pow-wow as described by Dr. Bernard Hoehner (designed by Monica Magtoto, magtotoart.com).*

of specific animals. Those woods, hides, and other natural materials are symbolic of the relationship between human beings and the environment of which they are a part. If the sound of the drum may be heard as the sound of those natural elements then that sound is not just a sound to motivate dancers, it is the sounding of the relationships between human beings and the world around them, reminding pow-wow participants that we—human beings—do not live in control of or apart from but very much in relation to and as part of the world. These ways of thinking illustrate the importance of the drum to a pow-wow and explain its placement at the center.

The male singers who sit around the drum represent the second circle of the pow-wow. The male singers around the drum have the responsibility of supplying the "heartbeat" of the pow-wow. By striking the drum they sound the relationship between human beings and the world of which they are a part. In order to respect that relationship, singers must take on the responsibility of singing and behaving "in a good way." "In a good way" is a phrase heard at many Native events and, as with many elements of pow-wow practice, there is no one specific "good way" but there are aspects of singer comportment that I find to be intertribally shared. For many singers, a good way begins with a commitment to sobriety, as it is often considered extremely disrespect-ful to sing while under the influence of alcohol and/or drugs.

State of mind is also an important part of male singer behavior. I remember asking Dr. Hoehner to explain why Northern Plains sing-ers sing as high as they do. He responded that Northern Plains–style singing was meant to emulate the cry of a newborn baby. As a younger man I was not always clear on the significance of that image but after the birth of my daughter, I had a different insight. When my daughter cries she is communicating with me in a language without words. She is telling me she needs to be fed or she needs to be held and I have to be able to hear her and understand her needs in the moment. As a pow-wow singer, I have to communicate with that same emotional intensity. This is not to say that words are not important, it is to say that those words must be communicated with an intensity that draws listeners in and makes them pay attention to whatever is being communicated at that moment.

The female singers who stand behind the drum represent the third circle of the pow-wow, surrounding the singers and the drum. In my classes on American Indian music I find students regularly assume that women are made to stand behind the drum because their musi-cal and social role is less important than that attributed to men. As it was explained to me, however, women stand behind the drum out of respect for the power of their role as mothers. Dr. Hoehner described the women as encircling the male singers and the drum in the same way that a pregnant mother encircles her baby. The place of women within the four circles as explained here should not be read then as a gendered slight but instead as a recognition of the balance and complementar-ity (Diamond, Cronk, and Rosen 1994) between men and women in the activity of producing music at a pow-wow.

> **ACTIVITY 2.3**   *Do a search for female pow-wow drummers or all-woman drums on the Internet. What sort of opinions on gen-dered space do you encounter? Make notes on the sites (and the URL) so that you can compare what you found with what your classmates found. Where do you stand on the issue?*

At the end of the previous section I mentioned that the subject of female pow-wow singing groups has played a defining role in shaping recent pow-wow practice (for example, see Hoefnagels 2012). Speaking for myself, my first experiences with pow-wow singing came in the context of Dr. Hoehner's Blue Horse Singers, a drum group in which women and men sat and sang. My own drum group, the Sweetwater Singers, is run in the same fashion as the Blue Horse Singers. Taking Dr. Hoehner's example, my drum group understands that the social relationships between men and women in pow-wow drum groups are represented in many different ways, reflecting individual, tribal, and intertribal influences, and women exercise their own agency in negotiating those influences in order to make music. For every drum group that gives women the choice to sit or stand another may choose to enforce rules that men sit and women stand. The issue, at pow-wows and in classroom discussions, comes in the interpretation of the rationale behind these decisions. In some cases the rules restricting women from sitting at the drum can be traced to tribal historical precedent and, in other cases, historical precedent may be used as a rationalization for **misogyny**.

While I may choose to believe in the social relationships of the four circles, it is equally valid for the young women who take my class to gravitate immediately toward the opportunity to sit down at the drum, as it is a matter of gender equality. The ability to sit and sing is not just a matter of music making—it is a powerful, empowering act with an enormous amount of cultural capital. It makes sense to me, in a culture of intertribal exchange, that women and men should have the opportunity to experience sitting at the drum. That experience also entails the discussion of different perspectives on the subject of female and male sociomusical roles around the drum so that men and women may come to their own personally relevant and meaningful understanding of pow-wow music performance. This is the core of the positive change brought about by discussions of female pow-wow singers: the space to think about why individuals pow-wow in the way they do and the space to consider changing those pow-wow protocols if necessary to meet the needs of local and national communities.

The dancers and other community members who come together at a pow-wow represent the fourth circle of the pow-wow, encircling the female singers, the male singers, and the drum. The question of what constitutes pow-wow dance at this moment in time is a very complex one since in the San Francisco Bay Area it is possible to see pow-wow dance, *danza Azteca*, California Indian dance, and guest dancers from other Indigenous nations participating at a pow-wow. My own sense of pow-wow dance styles falls into the following eight categories: Women's Cloth, Women's Buckskin, Women's Jingle, Women's Fancy

Shawl, Men's Southern Traditional, Men's Northern Traditional, Men's Grass, and Men's Fancy Dance.

ACTIVITY 2.4   *In order to get a sense of what pow-wow danc-ing looks like, do Internet searches for available pow-wow video excerpts using the dance style names listed above.*

Space does not permit a thorough discussion of each of these styles, so readers are encouraged to refer to available sources for detailed infor-mation (for example, Browner 2002; Ellis 2003). Primary attention will be paid here to the musical component of the pow-wow. Early ethno-graphic accounts of Native American dancing in conjunction with con-temporary research provide a presently available foundation from which to understand pow-wow dance styles, so I have chosen to interview four dancers who represent different men's and women's styles in order to understand their individual reasons for taking on the responsibility of their particular style. Those interviews will be featured at the end of this chapter.

The importance of pow-wow spectators should not be taken for granted in the context of the four circles. Far from simply being an audience, spectators fulfill a variety of roles in the process of help-ing to sound community. Pow-wow spectators, dancers, and singers all contribute to the economic potential of a pow-wow by exercising or not exercising their purchasing power. In addition to music, dance, and socializing, a large part of pow-wow culture revolves around ven-dors who sell arts, crafts, food, and other items. Pow-wows with small audiences often have trouble attracting vendors, who try to pinpoint pow-wows with large audiences in order to maximize their profits. Spectators, therefore, play an important role in the economic health of a pow-wow.

That economic health is not only a matter of capitalism but also of donations. At some pow-wows local community members may ask the assembled spectators for help with medical bills or assistance with gas money for a drum or dancer who came from a long distance. To honor that request a blanket dance will be held where a large blanket is placed in the pow-wow arena and a drum is asked for a special song. Spectators are invited to help the person or cause in need by placing whatever donation they can on the blanket. That money is then taken up and given to the requestor. The spectator thus plays a vital role in the sounding of pow-wow community through their participation as a consumer and also in terms of public donations.

THE ROLE OF A SINGER

Having located the pow-wow in time and space and place, we may now turn to the role of the singer and the many different qualities that define a singer's musicianship. Dr. Hoehner spent an enormous amount of time teaching me and others about the *responsibilities* of a pow-wow singer. For example, a pow-wow singer is expected to sing not for himself or for the accolades he receives but for his community. Without the singers, the dance cannot take place. A singer is not meant to take advantage of that relationship for his own gain. Instead a singer is supposed to give selflessly of his time and talents for the health of the communities the singer serves through his music.

Christopher Small's point that music is a social activity is apt in the case of pow-wow music for a number of reasons. While singers occasionally sing **solo**, at pow-wows you are most likely to see large groups of singers gathered around a drum or singing as part of a group of hand drummers. Once a drum "sets up" at a pow-wow, that drum, according to Dr. Hoehner, is expected to stay for the entire day, making the commitment to stay for the benefit of the dancers and the pow-wow as a whole. So, pow-wow music is not just a performance, it provides a sonic foundation for the larger social activity of the pow-wow.

When I began learning how to sing from Dr. Hoehner, I was not allowed to use **staff notation**. He required that I learn the music by ear, with the help of a tape recorder. I developed a routine to record our practice sessions and then sing along with that tape to memorize the songs. Dr. Hoehner would also give me tapes of his favorite groups and ask me to learn songs from tapes, a process that also helped my aural memorization skills.

ACTIVITY 2.5 *What is the difference between listening to music and hearing music? How is the kind of listening Dr. Hoehner taught me different from or similar to the kinds of listening you do in your everyday life?*

The most difficult aspect of learning Northern Plains style pow-wow music (CD tracks 1, 2, 4, 6, 7, 8, 9) was learning to produce the high-pitched tone characteristic of the style. The sound of Northern Plains pow-wow music can elicit all manner of reactions from first-time listeners. Former students have described the music to me as "warlike," "violent," "harmonized yelling," and "dissonant cacophony." While these descriptors may be valid for a first-time listener, as you continue reading and listening in this chapter, ask yourself the following quesion: What is it about the sound of Northern Plains pow-wow music, and pow-wow music in general, that might cause a listener to associate it with such descriptions?

> **ACTIVITY 2.6** *Listen to any of the pow-wow listening examples (CD tracks 1 through 9) and make note of the imagery that comes to mind as you listen. What do you see when you hear this music? Discuss your responses with classmates. Where do you think those types of imagery come from?*

WHAT'S GOING ON?

While every pow-wow is unique and run according to its own set of tribal-specific and intertribal rules, there is a somewhat standard order of events that characterizes most pow-wow agendas. The following descriptions of those events will assist you to understand what is transpiring within the dance arena when you attend your first pow-wow. For more information on many of the drum groups mentioned in this chapter, please see the Resources section at the end of this book.

Gourd Dance
Gourd dance is derived from Southern Plains military society dancing (Ellis 1990; Lassiter 1998, 99–115). Gourd dancing is not a contest dance category—only members of specific gourd societies and their invited guests can dance it. As such it is not technically a pow-wow dance style in the way that the eight categories listed for you earlier are. It has become ubiquitous at many pow-wows as a means of purifying or cleansing the dance arena before the pow-wow "officially" begins for the rest of the day ahead. This cleansing takes place via the gourd dancers' special status as returned warriors.

Gourd dancing is an important reminder of the influence of military societies on pow-wow music and dance. Depending on whether your community has local gourd societies, you may or may not see gourd dancing locally in your area. If you are present at a pow-wow for gourd dance it is sometimes common to hear the master of ceremonies request that no pictures or videotaping take place. This prohibition again refers back to the sacredness of this dance for many pow-wow people and should be respected if requested.

Grand Entry

Following the gourd dance, the **grand entry** marks the beginning of intertribal dancing at a pow-wow. All the assembled dancers enter the arena in a specific order (for one example see Browner 2002, 90), presided over by the **arena director**, whose responsibility it is to oversee and adjudicate pow-wow protocols.

As you will see throughout this chapter, pow-wow songs narrate the events taking place within the dance arena. In the case of grand entry, singers will sing about coming to dance and having a good time, as seen in the lyric excerpt below from Elk Soldier's grand entry song entitled "Hoka Hey" (CD track 1). The song begins with the voice of the master of ceremonies asking the pow-wow spectators to rise and remove their hats before the lead singer enters with the lead, sung with **vocables**, and then the A section, which includes words in the Dakota language. The words are repeated during the song's B section and the whole form of lead, A section, and B section is repeated in what is called a **push-up**. The voice of the master of ceremonies continues throughout the excerpt, explaining the significance of the different dancers as they enter the arena.

"HOKA HEY" BY ELK SOLDIER

	Translation:
Tȟéhaŋtaŋhaŋ wahíyelo	We came from afar.
Hókahey! Eš wauŋči ptaȟwá	Let's go. Are we going to dance?

Figure 2.3 provides visual representations of the differences between Northern and Southern Plains pow-wow song forms.

A push-up is loosely equivalent to the concept of a verse in Western music. You might also think of a push-up as a full repetition of a pow-wow song **melody**. I break down that large melody into two smaller chunks that I think of as the A and B sections. So, a full repetition of a pow-wow song would feature a "lead," sung by a solo voice, followed by the "second," or the A section, which is a response to the lead by the rest

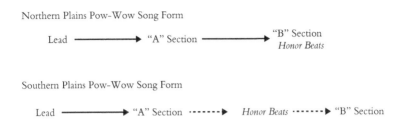

FIGURE 2.3   *Visual representations of Northern and Southern Plains pow-wow song forms*   *(designed by Monica Magtoto, magtotoart.com).*

of the assembled singers. The B section normally reworks some variant of the A section melody. You will always know when you have reached a new push-up when you hear the sound of the lead singer singing the song lead again. The only time you will hear a solo voice at a pow-wow drum is when the lead is sung.

You may also find it useful to keep track of push-ups by listening to **honor beats**. Honor beats, or "hard beats," take place during the B section of a Northern Plains pow-wow song, while in Southern Plains songs they divide A and B sections. I represent this by using solid lines in Figure 2.3 to indicate the discrete sections of a Northern Plains song and by using dashed lines to indicate the flow between A and B sections in a Southern Plains song. Upon hearing the honor beats dancers in the arena will acknowledge the drum by raising their dance fans, bowing toward the drum, or other movements. Dr. Hoehner taught that these beats are meant to remind all pow-wow participants to keep good feelings inside while dancing and to respect the drum.

There are many different ways to visualize pow-wow song form. Some scholars have categorized pow-wow songs as "incomplete repetition" (Powers 1990, 117), due to the fact that the lead or opening call is interrupted by the response of the full drum group. What is most important is that you are able to hear the moments diagrammed in Figure 2.3 as a way of keeping track of pow-wow song form and counting the number of push-ups in a given song.

Vocables are syllables used in pow-wow singing to convey a melody. While vocables may not have direct linguistic meaning, it is important to note in the case of pow-wow singing that well-sung vocables are heard as encouraging the dancers to dance and have a good time and so they do perform a communicative function. "Hoka Hey" uses a **straight beat** for the foundational drum rhythm. Readers with backgrounds in Western music theory might be tempted to parse the beat or pulse into groups of two or four in order to try and understand the rhythmic structure of the song. While this is a good way to get acquainted with pow-wow drum rhythms, I would also encourage you to think not in groups of two or four but in breath lengths. How many beats does it take for a singer to sing a musical **phrase** before they take a breath and begin another phrase? This kind of listening will give you multiple senses of how pow-wow music fits together.

Flag Song

The grand entry concludes after all of the dancers have made their way into the arena. At that point, an elder or honored guest attending the pow-wow is invited to give a prayer. This prayer refers back to the sacred component of pow-wow participation and asks for a good day, for good feelings, and a good time to be had by all. The prayer may be given in an Indian language, in English, or in a combination of both.

After the prayer, the master of ceremonies then calls upon the host drums for a **flag song** and **victory song** in order to post the colors that led the beginning of the grand entry procession. Flag bearers lead grand entry processionals into the arena. The responsibility of carrying in a flag at the beginning of grand entry is considered an honor, and veterans are often selected given their service and status. The number of flags leading a grand entry can vary from community to community; in my experience growing up, the most commonly seen were the United States flag (Stars and Stripes), the Prisoner of War/Missing in Action flag (POW/MIA), and the Eagle Staff. Other pow-wows may bring in flags from other nations, state flags, and flags representing the individual branches of military service. The flag songs and victory song are sung to respect these flags and the sacrifices symbolized through their presentation.

The flag song on CD track 2 is sung by the Porcupine Singers in the Lakota language and was recorded in the late 1970s. This song provides an opportunity to talk about the role of translation and interpretation in understanding pow-wow songs. In this particular case, different meanings can be understood by referring to the album liner notes and the translation provided by Dr. Hoehner. For example, the album liner notes indicate that the song is being sung to the "President's Flag," while Dr. Hoehner translated *tȟawápaha* as "eagle staff." This is not to say that one interpretation is right and the other is wrong, it is only to point out the depth of meaning to be drawn from these songs.

"LAKOTA NATIONAL ANTHEM (FLAG SONG) AND VETERANS' SONG," BY THE PORCUPINE SINGERS

	Translation (liner notes)	Translation (Hoehner/Alphin)
1) *Tȟuŋkášilayapi tȟawápaha kiŋháŋ*	1) The President's Flag	1) The Grandfather's banner/US flag
2) *Oíhaŋke-šni hé nazíŋ ktelo*	2) will stand forever.	2) Without end will stand
3) *Iyóhlate oyáte kiŋháŋ*	3) Under it, the people	3) Beneath it the people
4) *Wičíčaǧiŋ kte ča*	4) will grow	4) will grow and prosper, therefore
5) *Léčamuŋ-welo*	5) so I do this.	5) I do this.

This flag song too begins with the voice of the master of ceremonies requesting the song from the drum group. As opposed to the fast or straight beat of the grand entry song, the flag song features a much slower honor beat. The slower pulse of the honor beat provides a more reflective character that is not so much for dancing as it is for contemplation and reflection. The flag song concludes with a **ruffle beat** used here to indicate the conclusion of the song.

ACTIVITY 2.7 *Flag songs are sometimes referred to as "national anthems," as in the case of the Porcupine Singers' recording of the "Lakota National Anthem (Flag Song) and Veterans' Song," included on the accompanying CD. Articulate in a written paragraph what similarities and what differences do you find between the "Lakota Flag Song" and the national anthem or song of your home country?*

Northern and Southern Plains tribes have their own unique flag songs. In order to balance Northern and Southern Plains representation at large pow-wows it is common to have Northern and Southern drums share the responsibility of rendering the opening songs. So, if a Northern drum is requested by the committee or emcee to sing the grand entry then a Southern Plains drum will be given the responsibility of singing the flag and victory songs. This sharing is another articulation of the way community is sounded at a pow-wow that balances the sonic characteristics of Northern and Southern Plains singing. The Kiowa Flag Song (CD track 3) provides an example of a Southern Plains–style flag song to contrast with the previous Northern Plains example (CD track 2). Note the lower pitch of Southern Plains singing in contrast to Northern Plains singing. Head singer Bill Koomsa Sr. translated the song as "we are glad to hoist the flag because of the boys returning home" (White, Koomsa, and Toppah 1998).

To review, the flag song provides a moment of reflection at the beginning of the pow-wow to recognize the past and the present with an eye toward the needs of the future. While the pow-wow is a social event, the grand entry and the flag and victory songs that take place at the beginning of the pow-wow remind participants that there is also a sacred meaning to the event. The opening events may be seen and heard as functioning to provide a ceremony, straddling the line between sacred and secular, that reminds all participants to remember the many reasons why we are able to take advantage of these ways and to make sure they remain available for future generations.

Victory Song for Posting the Colors
Following the flag song, the master of ceremonies will request a victory song in order for the flag bearers to post their flags and to conclude the pow-wow opening ceremonies. Victory songs or veterans' songs, as was taught to me in a Lakota context, are songs that recount actions in warfare. After the victory song commences and has been sung for one or two push-ups, the arena director will signal to the flag bearers. The flag bearers dance up to the master of ceremonies stand and place the flag in holders, where they remain for the duration of the pow-wow until they are retired at the end of the day. The Porcupine Singers perform their victory song immediately following their flag song at 1:23 of CD track 2. The song is again sung in the Lakota language. Note that it narrates the action of the flag bearers dancing up to the MC stand to post the colors. This song transitions to a straight beat in order to mark the transition from a more reflective moment back to one intended for dancing.

"VETERANS' SONG (VICTORY SONG FOR POSTING OF THE COLORS)," BY THE PORCUPINE SINGERS

	Translation (liner notes)	Translation (Hoehner/ Alphin)
1) *É yuhá natáŋpi*	1) They are charging.	1) Having it they are charging
2) *Tȟuŋkášilayapi tȟawápaha ča*	2) The US Flag,	2) Grandfather's Banner (the US flag) thusly
3) *É yuhá natáŋpelo*	3) They are charging.	3) Possessing it, they go charging in
4) *Lakȟóta hokšíla, ohítika ča*	4) The Lakota warriors are brave.	4) Brave Lakota warriors, thusly
5) *É yuhá natáŋpi*	5) They are charging.	5) Displaying it they charge,
6) *Tȟuŋkášilayapi tȟawápaha ča*	6) The US flag,	6) Grandfather's Banner (the US flag) thusly
7) *É yuhá natáŋpelo*	7) They are charging.	7) They have it and go charging in

Intertribal Songs

Intertribal songs are sung for pow-wow social dancing, where dancers express their personal dance style by using a combination of set choreography and personal interpretation. Intertribal songs are usually sung with straight beats so they are most easily characterized by singing style: Northern Plains or Southern Plains. While many elements differentiate the two styles, I find that the best ways to differentiate them for the novice listener have to do with pitch and **timbre**. Northern pow-wow singing is characterized by a much higher overall starting pitch than Southern Plains singing. Because of the higher pitch there is also a sharper timbral quality to Northern singing, as opposed to the lower voices used by Southern singers.

On your compact disc you have examples of Northern and Southern Plains intertribal songs. The Northern style example (CD track 4) is performed by the Black Lodge Singers (Blackfeet) and the Southern style example (CD track 5) is performed by the Young Bird Singers (intertribal, Pawnee, OK).

ACTIVITY 2.8 *Listen to "Straight Intertribal" (CD track 4) by Black Lodge and "Road Warrior" (CD track 5) by Young Bird, paying attention to the different pitches and vocal timbres used by the singers. How would you describe the sounds of Northern and Southern Plains style singing to someone who had never experienced pow-wow music before? Listen again to CD tracks 4 and 5 and follow along with the diagram in Figure 2.3. Since the number of leads corresponds to the number of push-ups, how many song leads do you hear on each track?*

Contest Songs

In addition to intertribal songs, pow-wows will also feature contest dancing that utilizes a special repertoire of contest songs. Contest dancing has a long history in intertribal pow-wow culture that has contributed to the professionalization of pow-wow singers and dancers over time and has served as a vehicle for intertribal exchange on local, national, and international levels (Scales 2007). Contest categories are separated according to gender and sometimes age. So, for example, women dance against women in the cloth, buckskin, jingle, and fancy shawl categories but, depending on the pow-wow, golden-age women may dance separately from teenage women. Men dance against men in the Southern traditional, Northern traditional, grass, and fancy categories, but tiny tots dance separately from young men. Dance and singing contests are designed in a progressively difficult fashion so as to test both dancers and singers. You can hear this difficulty in "Home of the

Warriors" (CD track 6), a **sneak-up song** by Northern Cree. The song's lyrics are translated in the CD liner notes as "All right, start to dance and get down low!"

Sneak-up songs follow a very different form from intertribal songs. They begin with a ruffle beat, where each of the drummers strikes the drum to create a rumbling effect. The ruffle beat allows dancers to shake their bells and feathers in a stationary pose, creating a period of tension and release between the ruffle and then, after a pause, the transition to a straight beat. The straight beat can end with a formulaic **cadence** or

it can end quite suddenly, as in CD track 6. This pattern of ruffle and straight beat repeats three times. Instead of returning to the ruffle beat on the fourth repetition, the drummers keep the straight beat until the end of the song.

Dr. Hoehner taught that the sneak-up song form was originally used in the context of military society dances. This particular dance was used to honor a returning war party. The war party stopped three times on their way back to camp before finally riding home victorious. The sneak-up commemorates this by stopping three times before concluding on the fourth time round.

Keep in mind during a contest that the dancer is judged in part on their ability to stop and start in time with the drum. While many songs may share the same form, in the context of a contest the dancer must assume that the drums will save their most difficult songs to test the dancers. The dancers are in essence being judged on their ability to stop and start as if they know the song by memory without having heard it before that moment.

Other Social Dance Songs: Round Dance Songs
Round dance songs accompany another form of pow-wow social dance called "round dancing" that can and often does involve all spectators at a pow-wow, whether they are dressed to dance or not. By "dressed to dance" I mean being dressed in a specific outfit corresponding to a specific dance style at a pow-wow. I have included two Northern Plains round dances here, one sung in vocables by the Ironwood Singers (CD track 7) (Figure 2.4) and one sung in English—"Facebook Drama"—by Northern Cree (CD track 8). I will discuss each one individually below.

Depending on your location, round dancing, like other pow-wow dancing, is understood as emerging again from tribal ceremonial society dances conducted in a circle. Round dance songs then can reflect different forms that can sometimes be discerned through their beats. The Ironwood Singers' round dance (CD track 7) uses a large pow-wow

drum. In musical terminology the beat can be divided in groups of two with an accented second beat: 1 **2** 1 **2** 1 **2** 1 **2**. Dancers stand in a circle and dance to the left, moving ahead with their left foot on the accented second beat and following with their right foot on the first beat.

The head man and head woman dancers at a pow-wow normally lead the round dance. Once the head man and head woman dancers have established the beginning of the line for the round dance, other dancers who are dressed to dance will join them, dancing in a large circle in the arena, moving in a clockwise fashion. At some point as the dance develops, the master of ceremonies may invite all participants out into the arena. Once you hear that invitation as a spectator you may then enter the arena.

FIGURE 2.4   *The Ironwood Singers, 1979.*   *Photo courtesy of Canyon Records.*

    "Facebook Drama" (CD track 8) is performed using hand drums and a drumming technique originating from the performance practice of First Nations people in Saskatchewan and Alberta, Canada. A right-handed person playing a hand drum will hold the drum by its lacing with the left hand and hold the drum stick with the right hand. The drumhead is struck and then the head is muted slightly using the

FIGURE 2.5 *Northern Cree Singers, Honoring Singers and Songmakers Round Dance, Louis Bull Reserve, Hobbema, Alberta, Canada, 2003.* *Photo by Stephen Butler, courtesy of Canyon Records.*

fingers of the left hand. This adds a percussive buzzing or rattling sound to the beat that makes the sound very unique when compared to pow-wow drumming.

In the First Nations context, round dances take place independently of pow-wows and are held as stand-alone social events. Drummers gathering in the middle of the dance arena with individual hand drums and dancers form ever-widening circles around the singers, dancing with a similar shuffle step (Figure 2.5). "Facebook Drama" is included here due to the fact that it sounds generational perspectives on community and in this case that community is informed by the trials and tribulations of contemporary relationships mediated by social networking websites. Many round dance songs, regardless of location, have a teasing component and that influence is also audible here. The song begins with a vocable A section that leads into a B section featuring English lyrics.

"FACEBOOK DRAMA," MADE BY SHANE AND TWILA DION, PERFORMED BY NORTHERN CREE

I read your status last night,
You posted that someone else was holding you tight.
You shared it for all our friends to see.
I don't wanna go through this Facebook drama,
So I pressed "delete."

ACTIVITY 2.9 *"Facebook Drama" and websites like pow-wows.com illustrate the relationship between present-day pow-wows and technology. Make a list of bullet points and discuss with a classmate or friend. Does this relationship change the way you think about pow-wow music?*

Honor Songs
Honor songs are a general class of songs used during pow-wows to honor the accomplishments of individuals within a community. There are many reasons a person could be honored at a pow-wow. If a young person were coming out to dance for the first time, an honor song would be sung for that first dance. If a veteran were leaving for service or returning from a period away from home, a veteran's honor song would be sung to send them off safely or to bring them back into the community in a good way.

These songs serve as historical texts through which to understand not only how a community has been formed but also to understand the values important to the community. Many of the songs taught by Dr. Hoehner state that although it is difficult to be Native, one must always take courage and provide service to the community. Other songs recognize moments in history when Native Americans fought to maintain community, such as the Little Bighorn Victory Song (CD track 9). The song utilizes a straight beat and is sung in Northern Plains style.

LITTLE BIGHORN VICTORY SONG," BY THE IRONWOOD SINGERS

1) Kȟolá tókȟile, Kȟolá tókȟile?

1) Friend, where have you gone?

2) Kȟolá čéyapelo	2) Friend, they are crying.
3) Wazíyata kičízape	3) In the North they are fighting.
4) Kȟolá tókȟile, Kȟolá tókȟile?	4) Friend, where are you?
5) Kȟolá čéyapelo	5) Friend, they are crying.

This song is both a victory song and honor song. The classification of victory song refers to the fact that the song recounts deeds in warfare. The "they" referred to in this song are the 7th Calvary under General George Armstrong Custer. "They" are crying because Custer and his forces were defeated in 1876 by a combined force of Lakota, Cheyenne, and Arapaho during what is referred to as the **Battle of Little Bighorn**. That event will be discussed in detail in chapter 4. The song also functions as an honor song as it records the deeds of those individuals who fought against Custer that day and provides a way for contemporary generations to honor those acts. In this way, communities from the past are continually made part of the present in order to teach present generations lessons important to their futures.

THINKING ABOUT DANCING: FOUR REFLECTIONS ON POW-WOW DANCING

In this chapter I have described the pow-wow to you primarily from the standpoint of my participation as a singer and a scholar whose work focuses in part on pow-wow singing. That being said, pow-wow music is a form of dance music. In order to better understand pow-wows and pow-wow singing it is also important to think about pow-wow dancing.

As a singer, it is important to be attentive to the dancing taking place in the arena at all times. Good singers inspire dancers to dance their best all day by selecting good songs and performing them at the right tempo and pitch. As someone who does not dance at pow-wows, I rely upon the knowledge of dancers to guide my own understanding of pow-wow dancing and have been fortunate enough over time to meet and develop friendships with dancers who have helped me understand what it means to be a singer by sharing their sense of what it means to be a dancer. In this section, you will read the personal reflections of four pow-wow dancers in relation to their dance style. These reflections were solicited through interviews that took place in person and through email. It is my intention to present the interviews below with as little of my own written voice as possible in order to let each recollection stand on its own.

The intent here is not to detail the historical origins of every pow-wow dance style, as other scholars have already addressed similar issues (see, for example, Powers 1990; Lassiter 1998; Browner 2002; Ellis 2003; Shea Murphy 2007). Instead, I want to supplement preexisting materials with the voices and histories of contemporary dancers in order to introduce you to the subject of pow-wow dance through the unique experiences of dancers. Keep in mind that these recollections are individual and based on the personal experience of each dancer over the course of their lives. Other dancers in the same styles will undoubtedly have different recollections about their dance styles and that fluidity and individuality are part of the beauty of the pow-wow.

Michele Maas: Women's Jingle Dress

Michele is *Anishinaabe-kwe*, an enrolled member of the Red Cliff Band of Lake Superior Chippewa Indians. She works in the San Francisco Bay Area Urban Indian community, where she provides advocacy, prevention, and mental health services for Native American peoples living in an urban environment. Michele also speaks and offers presentations about issues facing the Indian community at the local and national level.

I was first introduced to pow-wow dancing in the 1980s. I was preparing to dance Jingle style when I was diagnosed with non-Hodgkins Lymphoma cancer in 2004. I received chemotherapy and also received care from a traditional Anishinaabe elder. After going through both western and traditional treatment I began dancing Jingle style.

I was told the Jingle Dress came from Whitefish Bay, Ontario. During about the 1920s an elder whose daughter was very sick had a vision. He dreamed the dress and that the dress would heal his daughter. Both he and his daughter were sick and they were both healed as a result of him taking action on his dream. He shared his dream with the people and the women sewed the dresses and helped his daughter around the arena. She was very sick and had to be helped the first time; each time round the arena she was helped by the women in the dresses, and each time she gained more strength. On the fourth time round she was able to complete the circle on her own. The Jingle Dress is also called a medicine dress for this reason. I am honored to wear this dress. The sound the jingles make when dancing is a prayer that someone is healed.

I think it's important for spectators to know that the dance by many jingle dancers is a prayer for someone and it's not just for show. I am honored to wear and to be among the women that wear the Jingle Dress.

Eddie Madril: Men's Fancy and Grass Dance

I am Pascua Yaqui, my tribe is from Southern Arizona and Northern Mexico. My parents moved from Arizona to the Central Valley of California in 1968 and a year later I was born. Both my parents are Yaqui, I am Yaqui. As I was growing up, in about 4th grade, 5th grade around 1979 in the Central Valley, I started participating in the Title IV Indian Education Project, which was a federal-funded program for American Indian Youth in schools for tutoring and cultural awareness. In that program I was able to learn a little bit more about the generic term "Indianness." We would have different people come in as guests, showing music or different arts or beadwork or dance. As an individual who was Yaqui but living in the Central Valley hundreds of miles from the homeplace of Pascua, our reservation outside of Tucson, I started gaining interest in this. We didn't go back home every year for ceremonies, so I was being taken under the wing of these different individuals teaching me these different dances. We asked back in 1979—and I was very proud of my parents for doing this—they asked permission from the tribe to do these dances because they are not from my tribe. It would be great to hear that a lot of people did that just to see that recognition and respect take place. It's not my place to ask other people to do that but I was very proud of my parents for doing that.

So I grew doing pow-wow dancing since about 1979, in 4th or 5th grade. It was a family experience, there were probably twenty kids that would come in and out of the program. It was a great time and a great place to feel secure in being Native around other Native people. It was a time to have pride in who we are, not who we were, and to congregate with other Native people and find security and comfort as a community removed from our original homeplaces.

I believe my first exposure to pow-wow was through the music on vinyl LPs and record players that the school provided. Eventually there was a group of young men who came out from the Fresno area; they were all Indian kids and they would come up once a week or twice a month and teach mainly fancy dance. 1979, 1980, 1981, that's the first time I started seeing that kind of stuff. In the midst of all that the gentleman who was directing the [Title IV] program, who was Seneca, he would put all of his kids—and there were about seven—and me in the back of his pickup truck with a big spare tire and a camper shell with nothing else in there, and we would all pack in and go to gymnasium pow-wows in the Bay Area. We were in the Central Valley but we would travel out to the Bay Area in the back of a cold pickup truck. We listened to a lot of old country music while my mom, their mom, and their dad drove us around to pow-wows.

I would say with my personality, I probably gravitated to it [Fancy Dance] but the truth is we're all so influenced by our environment and the people around us. Those kids were probably some of my first influences but the director

FIGURE 2.6   *Eddie Madril in fancy dance regalia.*   Photo by Eva Kolenko, courtesy of
Eva Kolenko.

had a couple of older boys who did fancy too. We all had to make our own outfits
and so the only outfit I knew how to make at that time and that I wanted to
because it had so many pretty colors was a fancy dance bustle. I think it was
more the influence of the kids from Fresno and the director's son who was about
five years older than me.

In the beginning years, it was about "let's just dance!" If they did teach me anything I think I was nine, ten so I probably wasn't listening because I don't remember anything being taught to us about origins or lessons. It was more "do these steps and stop on beat." "Do it again, do it again, do it again." "Keep on beat keep on beat!" It was more about doing the dance in the earlier years. As you build a commitment to it, other people start seeing you and giving you information from time to time. It probably wasn't until I was in high school that I heard stories about this dance coming a long time ago from Oklahoma people. You start hearing stories about the Wild West shows, you start hearing about people wanting to do something different after World War II. That's one of the beauties and burdens of living in the Central Valley and Bay Area; you have so many different tribal people telling you so many different things. Because I'm not Northern or Southern Plains—I'm Yaqui—I had to develop my own truth: if it's being done in the right way it should be making you a better person so you can share that goodness with other people. That's where the blessing and the prayer come without having to recite words.

My responsibility as a dancer is not to dance really good and win competitions. My responsibility is not to dance really good and make people like me. My responsibility as a dancer is that dance is prayer. Pow-wow should be prayer, pow-wow should be church. Dancing is not how you do move; dance for Indigenous people around the world is your fluidity and movement that comes from the environment. In your dance you celebrate that environment by showing the environment that you are a part of it. You are dancing for those who can't dance anymore or can't dance yet. My responsibility is to share those beauties with people so they can choose the one that makes sense to them and helps them become a better person. If time changes and people change, what shouldn't change is our heart and the great mystery of life as being beauty.

People throughout time have changed with their environment and have changed as a community. As time and people change, there is celebration in that change. For a pow-wow first-timer, they should see that a people who still know how to grow are not stagnant in the past. They are not going to keep an image of the past just because that's what people want. We're a community as a whole but we're made up of individuals as well and that's what makes us not so stagnant. A fancy dancer is a person who is participating and contributing to the whole. In the dance world today, different people play different roles going all the way back to dance societies. I like to say that fancy dancers bring liveliness, bring competition. It shows youth, it keeps you in shape. Fancy dance demonstrates change, it demonstrates artistry, it demonstrates the individual that is part of the whole.

Since 1984 I've had the burden and blessing of being able to do presentations on stage at schools, libraries, prisons, and colleges. Doing presentations *not just for performance, but for education, sharing the beauty of Native people but also making sure audiences know that there are many tribes and many different ways of dancing. Knowing this, I asked permission from the people I was dancing with, my brother Marcos and my other brother Tony, my family, a couple of other people, I asked permission: may I do grass dance for presentation purposes so that we can share something new? Aside from the many different dances that we do among us three and with guests, can I do this so we can tell another story? When that permission was granted I started doing grass dance but only for presentations, and I told myself I would not do grass dance at a pow-wow. I didn't want to disrespect anyone who had been taught that once you go fancy you can't go grass but once you go grass you have to stay grass. Once more people started finding out I was doing grass dance I started hearing that I needed to do it at a pow-wow. So I danced once at a pow-wow just to dance and everyone was fine with it. But I kept it at only dancing grass at pow-wows just to dance because people expect competition. Of course, that changed as well after some time and I would compete every once in a great while.*

Competing from 6th grade until I was around twenty-one or twenty-two, there was one point I found that I went to the pow-wow only to compete for the money and that's when I quit competing. I was dancing a lot but for about four-teen years I stopped competing. Eventually an elder grandma of mine gave me a dirty look when I told her I wasn't competing. I figured what her look meant was that I was an adult and mature enough to fight the temptation to dance only for money. So I started competing again and competing for fun. Sometimes I compete and dance really hard, sometimes I compete and I'm just having a blast. Neither one means I'm trying less or harder for the winning, it's just to dance just to dance. I get less tired and I dance harder.

When we do things with the right intention and the right spirit, that power comes through our bodies and you can dance on a sprained ankle or sick and you feel nothing. I dance competitions nowadays and I don't feel fatigued and tired like I used to. I'm not trying to dance hard, I'm just dancing hard because I feel good and I'm keeping prayer. Dancing good for the right reasons, having fun. If what I'm calling prayer is having fun and what I'm calling having fun is prayer then they are the same thing, having good intentions. That's what the church or ceremony of pow-wow is supposed to be, feeling good. Be that way completely from beginning to end.

Rulan Tangen: Women's Buckskin Dress
Rulan Tangen is an internationally accomplished dance artist and choreographer. She is the Founding Artistic Director and choreographer of DANCING EARTH Indigenous Contemporary Dance Creations. Rooted in cultural respect, her vision for dance is at the avant garde

experimental front of Native art expression in the United States. As performer and choreographer, Tangen has worked nationally and internationally in ballet, modern dance, circus, television, film, theater, opera, and Native contemporary productions. Her choreography, created from Indigenous principles of collaboration rather than hierarchy, explores the decolonization of theater premises and revitalizes Indigenous cultural practices.

When I was a teenager, dancing professionally with ballet and modern dance companies in New York, one of my mentors was the Apache/Mexican choreographer Miguel Valdez-Mor. We were working closely on early investigations of what was to evolve into Indigenous contemporary dance. He encouraged deeper exploration of our cultural roots and soon I found myself on a road trip to the Mashpee Wampanoag Powwow. The ancient night fireball games were memorable, as were the subtle complexity of the dances.

I initially wanted to dance fancy shawl, as a showcase for my physicality and technical skill that I had grown through my years of dance training, but my grandmother Geraldine declared that I had too much of that crazy contemporary influence in my life and wanted me to dance in the most ancient form of women's traditional dance. So, with characteristic determination I set myself to learn as much as I could by watching, asking, and dancing, dancing, dancing. She watched me practice the simple traditional women's step, the upright elegant posture and gentle pulse of the knees, with delicate variations of side steps, walking steps, and lifting of fan. I was learning to move with less effort, but evolving connection to the meaning. Although I had initially wanted to do a more physically expressive dance (grass dance actually being my favorite, but in those days very much beyond protocol for women), I eventually found that the repetitive rhythm of the traditional women's step revealed to me the essence of all movement, the heartbeat of the earth, the counter force up when you are down and down when you are up. It was a groundedness down into the core of the earth balanced with upper body poised as if hanging from a star in the sky, with quiet spiraling nuances all emanating from the central power of the spine.

It took several years of me asking Grandma Geraldine for an outfit and for this and for that. She usually responded by asking me to sweep, or clean the stove, or help her prepare food. I was taken aback, I saw myself as an "artiste," and a rather undomestic one at that. I know now that she was teaching me how to be part of a community, how to participate in a reciprocal way, to consider what I could give, and what was needed, rather than just what I wanted. Eventually she showed me how to make regalia.

My first buckskin dress! I envisioned a yoke heavy with complex beadwork patterns, but she said I should make something very simple and pure, a truly Native regalia without European influences, since I already had that in my dance life in New York. I labored hard for hours and created a beautiful buckskin fringed dress, with the natural contours of the animal hide still evident. And I was asked to give it away. This happened three more times, until I was convinced I would never keep my own regalia, and meanwhile she was showing me how to make grass dance outfits, and simple beadwork, moccasins, ribbon shirts, skillet bread, dried buffalo with choke cherries, and more. Finally, with my fifth grass dance regalia and fourth buckskin dress, she completed my outfit with hairties, belt, accessories, and welcomed me into the pow-wow circle.

There are many variations of women's traditional dance, as many as there are clans, bands, tribes, First Nations, and dream visioners. It is for each woman's personal connection with the living traditions of her culture. The materials of current life, such as cloth, beads, metal, are integrated as relevant to the ongoing manifestation of culture, which stays vital and evolving. Competition dance thus is more of a way to show pride, and dance in a circle of women, with regalia being seen from every angle, as living art in motion.

Each vision should be witnessed with respect, as a beautiful embodiment of each woman's relationship with her culture, in that moment of time and place. I feel that dancers should be mindful of this respect for themselves, in how they carry themselves during these times, when they are representing their ancestors. Even pow-wows, which are essentially intertribal socials, are a time to remember how to behave in relationship with each other, using words and thoughts in a kind and positive way, and behaving in reciprocity, from a foundation of respect for self-determination and sovereignty.

Between dancers and with the guests of a pow-wow, I would love to see the return of this reciprocity. A drum group comes to a pow-wow—let there be tobacco placed on the drum. Host tribes step aside to allow visiting dancers to "win" competition honors, while they show generosity through offering feasts and giveaways. Pow-wow prizes, how about Pendletons and plumes? Dancing for the honor. You like someone's outfit and want to take a photo, what about bringing them a gift? These are some of my ideas about the details of interactivity at a pow-wow, to revitalize a sense of relationship-based culture, which is at the traditional essence of these gatherings.

Marcos Madril: Men's Northern Traditional

I'm thirty-four years old and I've been dancing for about twenty-eight, twenty-nine years. Since I was about five, six years old I started getting introduced to pow-wow. I grew up around it, my mom would take me to a pow-wow, she would sit me there and I'd sit there and watch. I used to fall asleep right next to the speaker, right next to the drum groups, it was that comforting sound. We just grew up around it, I was there all the time. My mom and my dad, it was a family thing, we would just be there with the family. A lot of people end up asking "what is pow-wow?" For me person-ally it's just family, it's like a family reunion all the time, you have a lot of extended families all the time.

My mom used to run the Title IV program out there in Tracy [California]. She would conduct crafts, have kids come in, have other Native Indian families come over and contribute. We would eat, end up doing crafts, learned how to do beadwork and all kinds of feather work. And then dancing, people would try to practice their dancing. And teaching other people that would come and want to know what was going on with the pow-wow, so we'd end up teaching them how to dance here and there. Ed, my older brother, he was about thirteen and he met this Lakota gentleman Tony Fuentes. He ended up bringing Ed along and they'd go and do pow-wows and I'd just be there, a little kid. We would also take dance practices at Barbara Slice's house in Tracy. We'd go over to her house, Tony was good friends with her, we'd go over there and dance at the house, practice.

Men's Northern Traditional…I was five, six years old when Ed asked me, "do you want to dance at a pow-wow? What style do you want to dance?" I said "yeah, Northern Traditional." It was just something that connected to me, clicked with me. He ended up helping me out by going and asking different people what was right, what was proper. With us being in pow-wow my mom called back home to our tribe and asked the elders down there if it was OK that we danced this style at a pow-wow. They didn't have a problem with it because we're young boys and we just want to learn, get out there. So it was around six years old when I started getting my outfit together. People were helping me, I was borrowing roaches and people were giving me feathers to help me out. That's where it came in; I've been dancing ever since.

From there it was just a learning experience. Learning, being out there but then understanding, being given little snippets here and there from people. It's not material things, it's knowledge to understand Traditional dancing. Warrior dance, something to be respected, you're supposed to go out there and you're supposed to be dancing for the old warriors and the ones who are fighting right now in the military. When you do dance you dance for your elders and the ones who are coming up to teach them. That's my conception of the outfit.

People tell me the stories where it comes from, Northern Plains, where it's a storytelling dance. You're looking for tracks, you're looking for other ani-mals, you're looking high and low. You're looking for other warriors, when you encounter other warriors in a battle, or if you have a fallen warrior in front of you. Counting coup, go up and tap and just let them know that you came that close. That's what's been given to me.

In my dance style, when I dance, me personally, I'll throw different dance moves in there from what I've seen from older gentleman to honor other people, different dance styles. Just kind of throw a little dance move there for them, like I said it was just a lot of prayer, you're supposed to be praying for all these people. It's about understanding the spiritual aspect of everything because dancing with nothing but eagle feathers, it's a lot of burden and responsibility to carry that. With all the eagle feathers I treat them like family, treat them with respect because you have to treat yourself with respect. Understand that there is a lot of spirituality and prayer behind that outfit. Everyone is always coming up to me, "Can I feel that? Can I touch that? What kind of feathers are those?" And they just start gabbing and pulling, people end up crossing that barrier but I don't do that to anyone's hair or shirt or glasses.

A lot of people get that misconception that we go out and shoot birds. There's a lot of that, everyone thinks that we go out and we shoot birds and we get all these feathers, which is wrong because they are all on the endangered list. When I was little I ended up dancing with a hawk bustle, which I think is proper. Hawk bustle here in California, they revere it, the hawk feathers and turkey feathers as a lot of Natives do with eagle feathers. They're smaller feathers but for a younger person to be dancing with eagle feathers, they might not be ready yet. When I was around fifteen, sixteen, that's when I got my first eagle bustle. When I got the feathers they were handed down to me by Tom Phillips [Kiowa pow-wow emcee, dancer, and singer] *and from there I knew I had even more responsibility. Not only am I dancing for everybody, I'm actually dancing for him specifically because he gave me those feathers, so it was more of that responsibility. Those feathers from that bustle, I have them stored. The bustle that I have now is feathers that I got from Fish and Game* ["Fish and Game" refers to the National Eagle Repository established by the US Fish and Wildlife Service in the 1970s. For more information see http://www .fws.gov/mountain-prairie/law/eagle/] *and from a family member down in Salinas who had me take care of them. When you do get those feathers it's a gift. It's a gift from beyond us. It's understanding how to take that and pray on it when you receive that gift.*

It comes back to that responsibility when you are dancing with them, how you take care of them, how your pray with them, how you bless them, who you're thinking about, who's in your family to help you with that. That's the thing, when I'm getting dressed I like complete solitude. I'm sitting there putting everything on and I'm thinking about everybody, things that have been given to me, where they come from and making sure that I'm OK when I go out there to dance. People will come up before Grand Entry and ask to take a picture but no, not right now. I'm just trying to make myself right. I'm OK, my family is OK, and the community is OK when I go out there to dance, keep that balance.

THINKING ABOUT COMMUNITIES:
ATTENDING A POW-WOW

Every pow-wow is put on by a **pow-wow committee**. The pow-wow committee designs an agenda for the pow-wow and invites the participation of various head staff members including master of ceremonies, arena director, **head dancers**, and **host drums**. The pow-wow committee will also interact with craft and food vendors in order to have those services available at the pow-wow. On the day of the pow-wow the public voice of the pow-wow committee is articulated through the master of ceremonies, or emcee. The master of ceremonies is the voice of the pow-wow (Gelo 2005). It is his responsibility to keep the event moving by providing explanations of the different dances, introducing honored guests, dancers, and making sure that all the spectators, whether they are Native or non-Native are kept aware of what is taking place in a respectful and informative way. The master of ceremonies is also expected to use his sense of humor to keep the pow-wow atmosphere from getting over-competitive and keep all participants in a good mood, having a good time.

Given the importance of the emcee as the voice of the pow-wow committee, my first suggestion for you when attending your first pow-wow is: when in doubt, always follow the direction of the master of ceremonies. You will be able to hear the master of ceremonies broadcast over the sound system at a pow-wow. If you are a spectator at a pow-wow and the master of ceremonies asks the spectators to stand up, you stand up, unless physically unable to do so. If the master of ceremonies asks you to remove your head covering, remove your head covering—unless keeping it on is part of your religious practice. By following the emcee's directions you are showing respect as a pow-wow spectator and taking seriously your role as part of the fourth circle of the pow-wow.

Another suggestion, which cannot be stressed enough and is probably more accurately described as a rule, is to attend your first pow-wow sober and not under the influence of alcohol or drugs. Most pow-wow flyers will always stipulate that a pow-wow is a drug- and alcohol-free event (Figure 2.7).

This prohibition is meant to recognize the destructiveness of alcohol and drugs in American Indian communities and to advocate for healthier communities. By attending in a good way—that is to say, sober—you are showing respect to the many individuals who are working everyday toward recovery from dependency issues. You are also setting a positive example, regardless of whether they are Native or not.

FIGURE 2.7 *Student Kouncil of Intertribal Nations (SKINS), 2012 pow-wow flyer.* Designed by Ashley Richards, courtesy of SKINS.

While all of these rules may seem daunting, it is important to remember to have a good time. When you go to a pow-wow, think of yourself as entering someone else's home or, in the case of the intertribal interactions that have shaped contemporary pow-wow practice, it might be more appropriate to say you are entering into many different homes all at the same time. A pow-wow is a system of interrelated Native communities that is sounded into being by social interaction. In this case we have focused primarily on the creation of communities accomplished through pow-wow music performance.

The beauty of the musical practices discussed here is that they have served successive generations since at least the late 1880s and will continue to serve future generations. The key to their survival is the fact that pow-wows and pow-wow music change every weekend during pow-wow season in response to the needs of dancers, singers, spectators, and community members. Pow-wow origin stories reflect the diverse narratives from which pow-wow emerges, but those histories are always coming into being and balance complex influences. The beauty of pow-wow as an intertribal Native American musical genre is that it is today as dependent upon historical knowledge of events like Little Bighorn as it is on facility with Facebook. These influences may seem disjunct but they are reflective of the globalized circuits through which intertribal Native American music travels today.

Intertribal Native American pow-wow music can be heard as the sound of communities. These communities are located by place (where the pow-wow takes place), function within the pow-wow (singers, dancers, vendors, spectators, etc.), and social function within the pow-wow community writ large (for example, differing conceptions of the role of veterans or women from one pow-wow community to the next). These communities interact to create the fluid, constantly changing nature of contemporary pow-wow experience.

CHAPTER 3

Sounding Revitalization: Intertribal Native American Flute Music

My first experiences with the Native American flute came by way of my interest in and study of Northern Plains pow-wow singing with Dr. Hoehner at SFSU. After a Blue Horse Singers rehearsal in the early 1990s, Dr. Hoehner asked me if I had had any experience with what he called the "cedar flute." At that time I was aware of the Native American flute through commercial recordings by R. Carlos Nakai (Navajo, Ute) and I explained that I had no other practical experience with the instrument. Dr. Hoehner responded that if I wanted to learn how to sing it was also important to learn how to play the flute, as flute music from his Lakota cultural standpoint was related to vocal music. A few days after that rehearsal, Dr. Hoehner brought his own flute to campus and proceeded to show me two songs from his own repertoire. Rather than point me toward one player or another as an example of how to play, he encouraged me to listen to a wide variety of flutists and to find a personal style from those experiences.

Looking back on my participation in Native American flute music as a listener, researcher, and performer, there are resonances with my participation in pow-wow music. Key among those is the manner in which Native American flute music balances tribal specificity with intertribal exchange to make audible the diversity of Native American music performance and identity. This chapter will examine that same balance between tribal and intertribal as heard through Native American flute music, emphasizing the theme of sounding revitalization (Levine 1993).

After situating the concept of revitalization as it relates to intertribal Native American music, you will return to the concept of origin story through a flute origin story shared with me by Dr. Hoehner. You will then examine the revitalization of the Native American flute through the work of a select group of flutists active since the 1970s. I have chosen to begin with that time period since it marks the moment when flutist Doc Tate Nevaquaya (Comanche) released the first commercial recording of Native American flute music. His recordings reintroduced the Native American flute to audiences and built a lineage of performers whose output has contributed to the instrument's current popularity, including Tom Mauchahty-Ware (Kiowa, Comanche), Kevin Locke (Lakota), R. Carlos Nakai, and Mary Youngblood (Seminole, Aleut). The accompanying recordings are arranged in chronological order so I will discuss each flutist in that same order.

REVISITING NAMES:
WHICH NATIVE AMERICAN FLUTE?

The term "Native American flute" is somewhat problematic, in that it is a generalization. As with our discussion of tribal naming practices in chapter 1, it is necessary to specify the type of Native American flute to be discussed here. While there are many different examples of flutes and whistles of varying design used by Native American tribes (Payne 1999, 1–6), the flute pictured in Figure 3.1 is defined by ethnomusicologist Paula Conlon as a "vertical whistle flute with external block" (Conlon 1983; 2002, 63) and has come to be known as the Native American flute or Native American Plains flute (Payne 1999).

The external **block**, or "bird," is tied using a piece of leather to sit on top of the anterior air chamber port and wall, leaving a portion of the distal mouth opening clear. The spacer plate, on which the bird sits, raises the bird slightly and creates a space for air to circulate underneath the bird that is regulated according to a performer's needs by moving the block forward (toward the finger holes) or backward (toward the mouth piece), uncovering more or less of the distal mouth opening. Proper block placement is necessary to maintain "brilliance of pitch…and will affect the **frequency** of the distinctive warble sound common to well-made traditional instruments when all finger positions are closed" (Nakai et al. 1996, 7).

The pipe body or variable tube is carved with a number of holes that, when opened or closed via finger pressure, lengthen or shorten the overall tube length, producing lower or higher pitches. A flute **key** or tonal center is therefore a matter of its overall length. Conlon notes that historically flutes were often measured to the length of their maker's arm, thereby making classification by key a matter of the maker's physicality

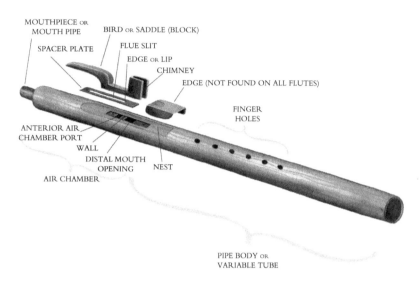

FIGURE 3.1 *Construction of Native American vertical whistle flute. Reproduced from* The art of the Native American flute, *1996, Canyon Records.* Courtesy of Canyon Records.

as much as design (Conlon 2002, 63). Flute makers today offer their instruments in specific keys, with G minor and F♯ minor being two of the most common. My primary experiences involve playing the six-hole Native American flute as pictured in Figure 3.1. In its standardized form the six-hole flute plays a minor **pentatonic scale**. In the key of G minor, that scale would be spelled as follows: G B♭ C D F G. It should be noted that while innovations over time have allowed for a certain degree of standardization, flute construction is still a matter of the maker's preference, and so every flute must in essence be learned as a unique instrument with its own tonal and performance qualities.

The ubiquity of the term "Native American flute" has been called into question recently by a number of sources, including Indian House record label owner and recordist Tony Isaacs and flutist Kevin Locke. Isaacs, renowned for conducting live outdoor sessions to record flute, pow-wow, and other Native American musics in their performance context, argues that "musically, 'Native American' has become a catch-all category for any music inspired by, derived from, in honor of, or performed by or for Native Americans, as well as including authentic traditional Indian music" (Isaacs 2005). Isaacs, speaking from his own generational perspective as well as referencing the perspectives of those he has recorded, prefers "American Indian" or "Indian" music to "Native American," as "Indian music is an expression of tribal aesthetic values" (Ibid.).

Kevin Locke has applied a similar distinction in the course of describing his concept of the American Indian flute versus the Native American flute (Locke 2011). From Locke's perspective, "American Indian" is a term created by the United States to refer to the Indigenous inhabitants of the land now referred to as the United States. Although it is a generalization, the term serves as a reference point from which one can specify unique tribal affiliations. American Indian flutes then are understood by Locke to be reflective of the tribal specificity of their makers and users. A Mescalero Apache flute will not and should not sound like a Standing Rock Lakota flute because those flutes will be constructed to reproduce songs and accompany languages that are unique to the areas from which they are created.

On the other hand, Locke hears Native American flutes as more ambiguous in character. Native American as a label, both federally and publicly defined, is potentially more global in scope and therefore could be indicative of any number of Indigenous cultures outside the boundaries of the United States. Locke also labeled innovations in flute construction, allowing makers to tune them to Western concert pitch, as a phenomenon unique to Native American flutes, while he situated American Indian flutes as the unique product of their maker's physiology and ear. So, while I have chosen to favor the designation of "Native American flute" here, I also recognize the importance of Isaacs's and Locke's comments as reflecting both the power of naming these instruments and the functional power of those names as articulations of tribal specificity and intertribal exchange.

ACTIVITY 3.1   *Revisit discussions of naming in chapter 1. How do you define "American Indian" and "Native American"? Pair up with a classmate or friend and discuss these terms. Once you reach a point where you have a sense of your mutual definitions, discuss Isaacs's and Locke's statements regarding the differences between American Indian and Native American flutes. Do you agree or disagree? Justify your answers.*

THINKING ABOUT REVITALIZATION

I have chosen to begin my discussion of Native American flute music with the revitalization of the instrument in the 1970s. Prior to this time, Conlon notes that the "United States government made a concerted effort to suppress Native American ceremonies and traditional cultural expression... the Native American flute... suffered a serious setback during this period and faded to a mere shadow of its former self" (Conlon 2002, 64). It was not until the 1970s, through the efforts of performers such as Doc Tate Nevaquaya, that the Native American flute began a period of revitalization leading to the present diversity of contemporary flute performance practices.

My definition of "musical revitalization" is informed by the work of ethnomusicologist Victoria Lindsay Levine. Her unique definition situates musical revitalization "a special kind of musical change":

> It is a strategy used by oppressed people to perpetuate their musical cultures in situations where an imbalance of social power exists. Musical revitalization is founded on individual conviction, and provides a unique opportunity to reshape, reinterpret, and redefine a musical culture. In addition, musical revitalization is articulatory in nature: it has to do with the way people use music to identify themselves, make sense out of their historical experience, and transcend social constraints such as the repression of traditional culture by the dominant group. (Levine 1993, 391–2)

This definition is relevant to the study of Native American flute in a number of ways. The position that revitalization is a strategy to continue musical culture in response to "an imbalance in social power" means that the study of the flute is not simply the study of a musical instrument. Much in the same way that pow-wow music is a social activity, Native American flute playing is also a social activity mediated by a variety of influences. As Conlon points out, one of those influences was and is the legacy of Native cultural repression by the US government. The revitalization of the flute now takes on greater social significance that can then be applied toward understanding contemporary transformations of the instrument.

Also important is Levine's statement that revitalization is "founded on individual conviction." The solo performance context of the Native American flute provides a unique opportunity through which to examine the manner in which individual musicians have taken up the Native American flute and the similarities and differences in the ways they have chosen to perform Native American flute music. This focus on individual agency within tribal and intertribal contexts means that the performers covered here are not going to sound the same and there is no reason they should. Levine notes that revitalization is "articulatory...it has to do with the way people use music to identify themselves, make sense out of their historical experience." Rather than hear the sonic difference between performers as markers of difference, it is more productive in the context of sounding revitalization to listen to these differences as signaling the depth and strength of the genre overall. The performers covered in this chapter, then, not only sound the revitalization of the Native American flute by learning and performing on the instrument, the sound of their performances in live and recorded contexts serves as a document of the many ways in which the instrument has sounded and may sound in the future. They may participate in the revitalization of the flute through performance but you perform an equally important function by listening to these performers and reading about their experiences, and helping to carry the music on.

NATIVE AMERICAN FLUTE ORIGIN STORIES

Having now specified the type of Native American flute to be discussed, addressed issues relating to its naming (American Indian versus Native American), and shown how the theme of sounding revitalization is relevant to the study of Native American flute, we can now turn to the subject of origin story. As in the previous chapter, the subject of origin story is important as it provides a means through which to understand the way the flute has sounded in the past and present, and may sound in the future. Native American flutes and precursor whistles were used in a variety of contexts from tribe to tribe, including hunting, medicinal, and ceremonial dance purposes. The block flute, however, is commonly associated with the theme of love and courtship in both the Northern and Southern Plains. Dr. Hoehner told the following origin story to me in the course of an early flute lesson:

> A young man had fallen in love with a young woman and the young man was trying to think of ways to draw the young woman's attention. One day, in the course of an elk hunt, the young man came upon a woodpecker in a tree. The woodpecker was busy making holes in a tree branch. As the wind blew and the woodpecker moved

back and forth over the holes he had made, the young man heard a melody. The young man recreated the branch as he had been shown by the tree, the woodpecker, and the wind and so the first flute was made. The young man took his flute and went to a private place to make a flute song for his intended. The young woman heard the song and recognized it as coming from the young man. She liked the song so much she paid attention to the young man and so the two began courting.

Ethnomusicologist and flutist Edward Wapp (Sac and Fox) explains the significance of the mention of elk in the context of Dr. Hoehner's flute origin story. For the Lakota, "dream societies were socio-religious organizations that were formed by men and women who had similar dreams or visions of a particular animal, deity, or one of the natural elements, such as wind or thunder" (Wapp 1984, 28). The elk was notable in the context of dream society membership because "the Elk Society...was comprised of men who had dreamed of the elk, and its members had special powers over women" (31). The "special powers" involved, among others, courtship as well as the healing of sickness (31). Dr. Hoehner's story can be read as an individual articulation of his knowledge of flute origin story that, through research, can be related back to larger cultural trends.

Those cultural trends are not limited to the influence of the mention of the elk in the story. Note that knowledge of the flute is not something that the young man simply finds and recreates for himself. It is through his attention to the world around him in the course of his hunt that he sees and hears the woodpecker in the tree. This teaches not only about the flute and courtship but also reinforces the interrelatedness of all things in the course of that search for love. Dr. Hoehner's origin story of the flute, then, is about much more than love between individuals; it teaches respect for the relations between individuals and the world around them that provided the flute as a means through which to court.

Dr. Hoehner's flute origin story is in keeping with the themes of revitalization as defined by Levine: it is an individual articulation that relates back to larger circuits of tribal knowledge while foregrounding Dr. Hoehner's expression of that knowledge. It should be recognized then that this is only one of many flute origin stories and provided as an introduction highlighting the subject of courtship from a tribal specific perspective. Payne (1999) provides a series of Southern Plains perspectives on the origin stories of the block flute.

NATIVE AMERICAN FLUTE PERFORMERS

Doc Tate Nevaquaya

Joyce Lee "Doc" Tate Nevaquaya (Comanche, 1932–1996) (Figure 3.2) was born in Apache, Oklahoma. Conlon highlights Nevaquaya's abilities as "a self-taught artist, flutist, composer, dancer, lecturer, and Methodist lay minister" (Conlon 2009). He performed and taught nationally and internationally and is regarded as a founding figure in the revitalization of the Native American flute through his performances on the first

FIGURE 3.2   *Doc Tate Nevaquaya, 1978, Oklahoma City, Oklahoma.*   Photo by *Verna Gillis, courtesy of Verna Gillis.*

commercial recording of Native American flute music, *Indian Flute Songs from Comanche Land*, released in 1976 (Wapp 1984, 50).

On the recording *Comanche Flute Music* (2004), Doc Tate recalls his first encounter with the flute as taking place in 1939 at a pow-wow. Lying awake at night listening to the sounds of the pow-wow, he heard love songs being sung in the distance and the sound of an instrument he could not immediately identify. As he grew older, he learned that the sound he heard was that of the flute and subsequently began a life-long career of study and internationally recognized performance on the instrument. Conlon writes that Nevaquaya "took it upon himself to approach [flute] players, win their confidence, and learn their songs. He also traveled to various museums…to examine their flute collections and listen to tapes of flute melodies" (Conlon 2002, 64). These actions reflect Levine's definition that revitalization is based upon individual conviction and provide a context through which to understand Nevaquaya's contributions to the resurgence of the instrument and genre.

Among his many innovations in the process of participating in the revitalization of the Native American flute, Doc Tate Nevaquaya is recognized for expanding flute technique and available flute repertoire (Wapp 1984, 51). Previous generations of flute players in the courting genre relied primarily upon vocal love songs as a basis from which to arrange their flute melodies. Older flutists would often perform a melody twice on the flute and then sing the love song twice, modeling their flute playing to some degree on the words to be sung in the vocal part of the song. Nevaquaya innovated purely instrumental forms of flute performance based upon arrangements of pow-wow social dance songs, hymns, and other vocal music. These songs, as Nevaquaya explains in the "Flute Wind Song Intro" (CD track 10), are intertribal in nature, as they emanate from pow-wows and other similar gatherings of many tribes. In the example of CD track 11, the arranged song was named by Nevaquaya as a "Flute Wind Song."

"Flute Wind Song" is an instrumental flute composition without words. Nevaquaya's playing shows the influence of earlier performers of Native vocal music in the way he uses his technique to emulate the sound of the human voice. Ornaments are accomplished by using the fingers to bend pitches and by using breath control to create **vibrato**. Doc Tate's vibrato in "Flute Wind Song" gives a sense of pulsation that propels the song forward and could even be heard as mimicking the sound of the wind for which it is named.

> **ACTIVITY 3.2** *Sing along with CD track 11 while trying to approximate the vibrato used by Nevaqauya in the performance. How does Nevaquaya's melody relate to earlier examples of Southern Plains singing (CD tracks 3 and 5)?*

Doc Tate Nevaquaya's artistic output helped initiate the revitalization of Native flute music in the early 1970s. That revitalization was articulated through a balance between the study of historical flute performance practice and the innovation of new genres of flute repertoire. This holistic approach provided multiple points of encounter for other players to experience Native American flute music and from which to develop their own personal styles. That diversity of approaches to the Native flute can be heard in the sounds of the many musicians who followed Nevaquaya, bringing the past into the present and future.

Tom Mauchahty-Ware

Tom Mauchahty-Ware is a Kiowa and Comanche flutist, singer, dancer, and artisan, born in Anadarko, Oklahoma. He is known for his involvement in multiple genres of Native music including flute, Southern Plains pow-wow singing and dancing, and the band Tom Ware and Blues Nation. He also leads his own Kiowa-Comanche dance group. Wapp notes that Mauchahty-Ware is a relation of Belo Cozad (Wapp 1984, 51). Payne highlights Cozad as "an early exponent of the [Native American] flute, [who] made many flutes in the late 19th and early 20th centuries" (Payne 1999, 8). Belo Cozad was recorded by the Library of Congress in 1940 and can be heard speaking and playing the flute on *A Treasury of Library of Congress Field Recordings* (Ping playlist track 1).

Mauchahty-Ware's first recording, *Flute Songs of the Kiowa and Comanche* (1978), can be heard as referencing the influence of Doc Tate Nevaquaya in that it contains arrangements of both historical and contemporary flute repertoire for that time period. Kiowa love songs and riding songs, a genre likened by Mauchahty-Ware to songs composed when riding in a car whistling to oneself (Mauchahty-Ware, as quoted in Hercules and Jackson 1999), are juxtaposed with arrangements of Native hymns and social dance music. Liner notes are provided, containing a Kiowa flute origin story, song descriptions, and statements from both Mauchahty-Ware and Indian House Records owner and recordist Tony Isaacs.

Mauchahty-Ware's performance style can be heard on his "Courting Song" (CD track 12). Liner notes indicate that the song began its life as a courting song and that, at the time of recording, it was also being used for pow-wow social dancing. The fluidity of song classification and performance context in this case speak to the idea that revitalization makes audible the different ways in which people use music to make sense of their history and identity. Mauchahty-Ware proceeds at a stately pace, contrasting the smooth high register of his flute with long notes emphasizing vibrato in the lower register. Ornaments are again used to convey the vocal quality of the original melody. Mauchahty-Ware's and Isaacs's decision to record live outside in the natural ambiance of Hog Creek, Oklahoma, adds another layer to the recording that introduces a sense of place into the listener's experience with the songs. Responding to Conlon's comments concerning government repression of Indian cultural expression, the sounding revitalizes Native lands as spaces within which musical performances can safely take place.

Wapp characterizes Mauchahty-Ware's concept as relating to "various aspects of love, rather than the love song itself" (Wapp 1984, 51). As mentioned in Dr. Hoehner's origin story, in a Lakota context the flute is perceived as a courtship instrument and those associations with love have played a large role in its contemporary popularity. An overemphasis on love understood as courtship endangers the future growth of flute music, as it limits the contexts in which the instrument can be played and heard. Mauchahty-Ware's concept of Native flute music plays the important role of expanding the concept of love from a single focus on courtship to include love as experienced between friends and family or between an individual and their god or creator. This revitalizes the function of the Native American flute and creates new performance contexts in which the instrument and its players can grow.

ACTIVITY 3.3 *How do you define "love?" Make a list of ways in which it is possible to narrowly and broadly define the concept of love.*

Kevin Locke

Kevin Locke is a Lakota and Anishinabe flutist, dancer, and storyteller from the Standing Rock reservation. He has recorded extensively since the early 1980s in solo, acoustic, and electric group settings ranging from orchestras to world fusion **ensembles**. Locke tours nationally and internationally as a lecturer at schools and universities and, like Tom Mauchahty-Ware, as part of his own dance ensemble, The Kevin Locke Native Dance Ensemble. In addition to his work as a performer and teacher, he has also recorded flute music for public television including appearances on the soundtracks for the Lakota language version of *The Berenstain Bears* (2011), produced in conjunction with the Lakota Language Consortium.

Although there are any number of recordings through which to hear Locke's style, I have chosen to examine "The Photograph" (CD track 13) from *Love Songs of the Lakota* (1982) due to my sense of the album's role in the revitalization timeline of the flute. It is similar to previous recordings by Nevaquaya and Mauchahty-Ware in that it presents a set of solo flute songs based upon Native American vocal music and, in this case, an all-Lakota repertoire of love songs. As *Love Songs* is also an Indian House Records release, Locke and Isaacs chose to record in the natural setting of Storm Mountain in the Black Hills of South Dakota. As with Mauchahty-Ware's recording, this decision to record live outside adds a level of natural ambiance to the recording and creates a sense of place within which to experience the music. The recording contains liner notes by Locke and Wapp as well as English translations of the Lakota love songs featured on the disc and explanations of the provenance of the flutes used by Locke.

Locke's style can be heard in his performance of "The Photograph". The recording begins with the sound of running water, indicating that Locke was recorded near a creek or other water source. While the words are not sung on the recording, a translation is provided that gives insight into the song. "The Photograph" is sung in the voice of a young woman speaking to a young man. The young man is leaving to join the military and, since the two will not see each other for some time, the young woman gives the young man a picture to remember her by while he is away. Locke's rendition proceeds at a fast pace and emphasizes a repeated ascending slide in the upper register of the flute. Locke also utilizes vibrato in the upper and lower registers of the flute, creating a sense of rhythmic propulsion. Dr. Hoehner taught a version of this song to me and provided the following Lakota lyrics and English translation. Wapp also transcribed a version of the song from a recording by ethnomusicologist Willard Rhodes with alternate Lakota lyrics and translation (see Wapp 1984, 176)

LYRICS TO "THE PHOTOGRAPH," AS TAUGHT TO JOHN-CARLOS PEREA BY DR. BERNARD HOEHNER

Itówapi kiŋ le yuhá na miksúya
he míya
Šičé itówapi kiŋ le yuhá na
miksúyaye
Théhaŋ owáyawa na wagniŋkte, šoš.
Šičé itówapi kiŋ le yuhá na
miksúyaye.

Take this picture and remember me by it
For I am going away and may never return

ACTIVITY 3.4   *Sing along with CD track 13 while trying to approximate the vibrato used by Locke in the performance. How does Locke's melody relate to earlier examples of Northern Plains singing (CD tracks 1, 2, 4, and 6–9)?*

Locke's liner notes contextualize the listener's encounter with Lakota flute music from his perspective as a Lakota flute player: "In former times Lakota women were closely guarded because of their position as 'the foundation of the people'. Men could earn the right to go courting only after establishing themselves as hunters and defenders of the hearth" (Locke 1982). Incorporating the social responsibility of courtship once again expands upon the concept of love to include tribal-specific perspectives sounded through flute performance. Recognizing a woman's power as mother and the importance of that role to the tribe, men are not allowed to court unless they similarly prove their worth to the life of the group. Having earned the right to court, a young man could compose his own songs or turn to the previously mentioned Elk Society: "It was believed that the elk had love power, and this power was passed to those who had dreamt of the elk. When used in this context, the flute becomes a medium for transmitting this power" (Wapp 1982). *Love Songs* can in this way be heard and read as revitalizing tribal specific understandings of, as Locke might put it, American Indian flute performance and specifically Lakota flute performance.

R. Carlos Nakai
R. Carlos Nakai (Figure 3.3) is a Navajo and Ute cedar flutist who began his career as a trumpeter and took up the flute in the early 1970s after

receiving the instrument as a gift. In the liner notes to the rerelease of Doc Tate Nevaquaya's *Comanche Flute Music*, Nakai places himself in the lineage of flute players by relating his experience purchasing that album in 1979 and discussing Nevaquaya's influence upon him. It is interesting to note that while Nakai was never able to meet Nevaquaya,

FIGURE 3.3   *R. Carlos Nakai, c.1997.*   Photo by John Running, courtesy of Canyon Records.

he highlights the importance of his recordings as revitalizing public interest—including Nakai's own—in the instrument. He also points out the importance of songs as carrying "the life experiences of countless generations of our ancestors, whose aspirations we are now responsible for carrying further into time" (Nakai 2004, 2). Relating his statement to circular time, flute songs revitalize the past in the present, but that encounter carries with it a sense of responsibility for future generations.

Since beginning his recording career in 1983 with Canyon Records, Nakai has released over thirty-five albums of flute music, ranging from solo recordings to small and large ensembles in the genres of world, jazz, and classical music. His solo albums are influenced by and in many ways pay their respects to the solo flute tradition of Nevaquaya, Mauchahty-Ware, and Locke. However, Nakai is equally known as a pioneer in the use of the flute as a fusion instrument, performing alongside musicians and instruments from around the world.

Nakai's *Earth Spirit* (1987) and *Canyon Trilogy* (1989) have both been certified as gold records, indicating 500,000 units of each sold. Like Locke, he has contributed to film soundtracks, including *The New World* (2005) and *Geronimo* (1993). His awards are also numerous and include seven Grammy nominations. Given the breadth of his catalog and influence, two examples of Nakai's playing are included here: "Shaman's Call" (CD track 14) from *Earth Spirit* and "Lake that Speaks" (CD track 15) from *Two World Concerto* (1997).

"Shaman's Call" is an example of Nakai's solo flute playing and is described in the liner notes as "a beginning prayer emulating the soaring eagle's call to the sky and earth" (Nakai 1987). While he does not directly refer to love songs, I locate Nakai's concept as similar to that of Mauchahty-Ware, in that his sense of the love communicated by use of the flute is not limited to courtship and can include many different expressions of that emotion. CD track 14 differs from previous selections by Mauchahty-Ware and Locke in that it was recorded in a studio and makes use of technologies such as delay and reverb to achieve a sense of ambiance. While this might change the feeling of place communicated in recordings by Mauchahty-Ware and Locke, it also allows Nakai the freedom to explore different uses of technology in the process of revitalizing the Native American flute, sounding the mobility and cosmopolitanism of Native Americans (Diamond 2005). Heard in comparison to previous examples, Nakai's style is characterized by an impressionistic use of ornamentation while still foregrounding the vocal qualities of the flute.

"Lake that Speaks" is the second movement of the *Two World Concerto*, composed by James DeMars. A concerto is an orchestral work featuring an instrumental soloist. The second movement is described in the liner notes as "impressionistic" in quality as the composer's intention was "to bring the forest and waters of his home in Minnesota to life" through the piece (Nakai and DeMars 1997). The flute, which has previously been heard playing within the limited range of its minor pentatonic foundation scale, is now transformed through DeMars's writing and Nakai's artistry into a fully functioning soloist in the orchestral context, able to perform melodies as complex as any of the Western instruments with which it shares sonic space. Nakai's performance here makes extensive use of cross fingerings to expand the range of the flute from seven to fourteen notes.

While Nakai balances the historical role of the flute player as an aural historian and culture bearer passed down through previous generations, he is not solely defined by it. This is not to say the flute players discussed here before Nakai are "throwbacks." If Doc Tate Nevaquaya had never recorded his music and in doing so found a personal balance with contemporary technology then the revitalization of the Native American flute may have taken a very different path and this chapter might never have been written! Nevaquaya, Mauchahty-Ware, Locke, and Nakai all embrace a certain fearlessness in recording their music and making it possible for listeners to experience it through commercial release. The tribal and intertribal perspectives they sound in performance add to the depth of flute repertoire and, in doing so, continually revitalize the sonic and cultural possibilities of the flute.

ACTIVITY 3.5 *Make a list of the similarities and differences between Nakai and his predecessors. Those similarities and differences could relate to performance styles or to your perception of their flute concept. Then, make a bullet point list of your observations to Nakai's solo performance on CD track 14 versus Nakai's orchestral performance on CD track 15. Does the use of the flute in an orchestral context change your perception of the instrument?*

Mary Youngblood
Mary Youngblood is a Seminole and Aleut flutist who, like Nakai, began her career as a classically trained musician before taking up the flute. In addition to her work as a recording artist and performer Youngblood has worked on a number of film soundtracks including

Aleut Story (2005), a documentary on the forced relocation of Alaska Natives from the Aleutian Chain during World War II. She is also active as a teacher and is the credited with cofounding the Northern California Flute Circle in 1994. Ethnomusicologist Beverley Diamond notes that Youngblood plays eighty types of flutes, including the block flute (Diamond 2002, 29).

Youngblood has become known for her status as the first Native American female flutist to win a Grammy award, in 2002 for *Beneath the Raven Moon* (2002). She won a second Grammy in 2007 for *Dance with the Wind* (2006). Her recognition through these awards created an important moment of revitalization and change in Native American flute music, as it challenged the notion of the flute as a man's instrument. While some may view this as detrimental to the preservation of the historical courtship tradition, Diamond highlights the fact that Youngblood plays her own compositions and in doing so "avoids appropriating traditional music" (Diamond 2002, 29). In this way, Youngblood has revitalized historical understandings of the flute in relation to gender and, in doing so, has created new performance contexts for the instrument.

Youngblood can be heard on CD track 16 performing "Beneath the Raven Moon" from her 2002 Grammy-winning album of the same name. Youngblood's liner notes (2002) contextualize her music as inspired by relationships experienced during one's life, locating her in the concept of the flute expressing love in its various forms. "Beneath the Raven Moon" is recorded in the studio and features a trio of flute, acoustic guitar, and cello. Youngblood's notes indicate that the flute used on this track was made by Chris Ti Coom from paduk wood and plays in the key of F. This information is important to flute students as it provides information on flute makers and makes playing along at home easier for those who wish to learn the song.

"Beneath the Raven Moon" makes audible the long history of flute playing since the 1970s. On one hand it is possible to hear the smooth vocal quality associated with flute playing discussed throughout this chapter. On the other hand, the flute melody is tightly and expertly arranged to fit the acoustic guitar and cello counterpoint. Her performance then is one in which the past is brought into the present and a potential future is sounded. That future is very real for Native American musicians in that it involves the revitalization of historical repertoires of music so as to make them relevant to contemporary audiences. In essence, that is what every musician covered here has done: expanded upon tribal-specific and intertribally shared knowledge of Native

American flute music through solo performance, orchestral settings, small group ensembles, recordings, and other formats not covered here.

ACTIVITY 3.6 *Previous examples in this chapter have characterized the flute in terms of its relationship to the human voice. While "Beneath the Raven Moon" is similar in this regard, the trio setting allows you to consider the ways in which the flute, guitar, and cello interact with each other as part of an ensemble. Listen to CD track 16 three times, paying attention to the musical roles of each instrument. How would you describe the interaction? Is there a soloist throughout or is the solo role shared by all instruments? Be prepared to discuss your observations with a classmate or friend.*

These artists have perpetuated Native American flute performance in the face of a historical narrative in which the flute, and other genres such as pow-wow music, came close to being silenced. Their musical output is shaped by individual and tribal-specific practices through which they make sense of historical experience and articulate their unique place in the world. While I have in this chapter formulated a particular timeline based upon influential recordings and the theme of revitalization, there are many other flutists who have also revitalized the instrument over time. John Rainer Jr. (Taos Pueblo, Creek, 1942–2011) was a highly regarded flute maker and performer, known for his use of synthesizers as part of his recordings. Phillip Charette (Yup'ik, French Canadian) has expanded Native American flute repertoire by arranging Yup'ik music for the Native American flute. These artists and many more make audible the revitalization of the Native American flute not by following one single practice but by sounding the same complexity and diversity as pow-wow music. The benefit to contemporary students of the flute is the opportunity to study tribal-specific and intertribally shared styles of flute performance and in doing so to understand the importance of each to the continued revitalization of the instrument.

CHAPTER 4

Sounding Activism: Native American Popular Music and the Occupation of Alcatraz Island

Of the many unique urban Native events taking place in the San Francisco Bay Area the Alcatraz Island Sunrise Ceremony, held for the past thirty-eight years on Thanksgiving Day morning, holds a special place in my memory, as it deepened my understanding of the continuing relationship between political activism and intertribal Native American music. I can recall attending my first sunrise ceremony as an undergraduate at SFSU. Ceremony participants board ferries at the pier on the northeastern edge of the city in the early morning darkness and ride north across the San Francisco Bay to Alcatraz Island. While Manuel de Ayala is credited with "discovering" the island and naming it *Isla de los Alcatraces*, or Island of the Pelicans (Johnson 2008, 2), Native American Studies scholarship on the island recognizes its use as fishing and hunting grounds by the Muwekma Ohlone (Leventhal et al. 2012) and as a navigational marker used by the "Coast Miwok, Pomo, Wintun, Wappo, Maidu, and Northern Yokut...when navigating the bay in their balsa canoes" (Johnson 2008, 1). Alcatraz is most commonly known through tourism and pop culture reference as an infamous prison site. While that history commonly emphasizes criminal figures such as Al Capone in the 1930s and Robert Stroud, the Birdman of Alcatraz, in the 1940s, American Indian Studies scholar Troy Johnson notes that the island's history as a prison dates back to the 1860s when it housed military and civilian prisoners, including many American Indians (Johnson 2008, 3).

Once on the island, participants walk up from the island pier to the parade grounds near the main cell house where the sunrise ceremony takes place round a large fire. California Indian history on the island is recognized and recounted for those present, as well as the history surrounding the occupation of Alcatraz Island. From November 20, 1969, to June 11, 1971, a Native American student group called Indians of All Tribes occupied Alcatraz Island in order to bring American Indian social, political, and economic concerns forward in the larger social movements taking place at the same moment in time, like the civil rights movement. Growing up in San Francisco and identifying in part as an urban American Indian, I was and am very influenced by the living legacy of the Alcatraz occupation. As a musician I was particularly interested in the ways that musicians and music were used to sound political activism from this period in time.

Thinking back to my first experience attending a Sunrise Ceremony on Alcatraz, I can remember riding the ferry to the sounds of live pow-wow singing and drumming taking place on the boat. The drum and singers were again prominent on the island as they led assembled participants up the hill to the parade grounds. Once the participants arrived at the parade grounds and the ceremony began, the drum shared the sonic space with the sounds of Pomo singing and clapper sticks. Over time, the Sunrise Ceremony has featured performances by many different singer-songwriters, including Floyd Red Crow Westerman (Dakota) and Jeremy Goodfeather (Iroquois). This combination of different tribal and intertribal influences and contrasting musical genres reinforced the idea that there are many different ways to sound Indian and also to sound one's personal sense of political activism through musical performance. Returning from my first Sunrise Ceremony, I wanted to learn more about the ways Native American musicians interacted with political activism through popular music.

That interest in Native American popular music, activism, and the influence of the Red Power Movement generally and the Alcatraz Occupation specifically has led to the present chapter. Whereas in chapter 2 you explored the sounding of communities through pow-wow music and in chapter 3 the sounding of revitalization through Native American flute music, this chapter proposes to listen to the sound of activism through Native American popular music around the time of the Alcatraz occupation. I will focus in particular on musical predecessors to the 1969–1971 occupation, as well as performances during the period of the occupation. While there are many theoretical means through which to observe and analyze the performance of activism through music, I have chosen to reference Diamond's concepts of "alliance studies" here (Diamond 2007). After outlining Diamond's thinking and its relevance to the present chapter, I will proceed to some historical background on

American Indian political activism leading up to the Alcatraz occupation and introduce various relevant musicians and ensembles, including Peter La Farge (Narragansett), Buffy Sainte-Marie (Cree), Floyd Red Crow Westerman, Redbone, and XIT. Selected examples have been made available to you, where available, via Ping playlist at https://c.itunes. apple.com/us/imix/intertribal-native-american/id553025235.

> **ACTIVITY 4.1** *As you read about and listen to the various artists discussed in this chapter, keep a listening journal, where you reflect on the subjects of sounding activism and circular time. In what ways do the soundings presented here help you to understand your past, present, and future in relation to intertribal Native American Music in the United States?*

THINKING ABOUT ALLIANCES BETWEEN MUSIC AND ACTIVISM

Diamond's "alliance studies" provide a structure through which to listen to the relationship between music and activism, as articulated by Native American performers in the 1960s and 1970s. The author bases her model on the idea that "we should regard musical practices *as* theory not as objects to which we might apply theory" (Diamond 2007, 169). I find that this resonates strongly with Christopher Small's statement, cited in chapter 1, that music is not a thing but a social activity. This emphasis on the music as social process leads Diamond to situate alliance studies as "look[ing] at ways that concepts and social relationships of the past are embedded in the present...track[ing] connections to places, or networks of people" (2007, 171). She highlights in particular the areas of alliances between performers and technology, access and ownership, citation, collaboration, and language (171). Following Diamond's lead, it is now possible to refine the theme of the present chapter: sounding activism through alliances. I will highlight this theme where relevant to the following artists and listening examples.

RED POWER ORIGIN STORIES

Like "pow-wow" and "Native American flute," the use of the term "Red Power" as a descriptor can have different meanings and associations depending on the cultural and generational perspective of the person using it. Rather than understand Red Power in relation to singular events or individuals, I find it more helpful to situate it as a part of a long historical narrative of Indian political activism taking place on reservations and in urban centers. It should be noted before moving on to a description of that timeline that the Red Power Movement did not end where this chapter concludes, at Alcatraz, but continued into the 1970s with events such as the Trail of Broken Treaties caravan in 1972 and the **Wounded Knee II** occupation in 1973 (Smith and Warrior 1996, 142–68, 194–268). Red Power at that time period was also not limited to the United States, as can be seen through events that took place in Canada, such as the 1968 blockade of the Cornwall International Bridge by the Mohawk and the creation of the Indian newspaper Akwesasne Notes (Johnson, Nagel, and Champagne 1997, 16). As this textbook goes to press, the #IdleNoMore movement in Canada is redefining the contemporary scope of Native activism and Red Power through a model that employs social media as an organizing and communication tool to circulate its message to the widest possible audience. Given my personal experiences around Alcatraz and continued interest in that event in popular culture, I am choosing to use that event as an organizing point around which to discuss sounding activism, but readers are encouraged to investigate these later events on their own and to continue listening for the ways in which music and activism continue to resonate in relation to intertribal Native American music in the United States.

While there are many ways one could formulate a timeline of Native political activism, I find it useful in my classes to trace it by paying attention to Native political organization in the twentieth century. The Society of American Indians (SAI) was formed in 1911, "with the purpose of establishing the first Indian-controlled intertribal organization" (Shreve 2011, 18). Founding members included physician Charles Eastman (Dakota), author Gertrude Bonin (Dakota), and physician and newspaper publisher Carlos Montezuma (Apache, Yavapai). The SAI was noted for its assimilationist stance toward American Indian affairs and, by 1923, it had eventually broken up due to internal conflicts between members on issues of religious freedom and citizenship (Kidwell and Velie 2005, 1). Following the disintegration of the SAI, the American Indian Federation (AIF) was formed in 1934, following a similar assimilationist-minded platform (Shreve 2011, 26–32).

That trend changed in 1944 with the founding of the National Congress of American Indians (NCAI). Historian Bradley Shreve notes, "where assimilation and acculturation had been bedrocks of the SAI and the AIF, the new intertribalism [of the NCAI] embraced cultural preservation, treaty rights, and tribal sovereignty" (Shreve 2011, 35). The NCAI was also instrumental in combatting federal termination policy in the 1950s, which sought to end the nation-to-nation relationship between the federal government and Native nations in favor of full assimilation into American society (Fixico 1986). Paul Chaat Smith (Comanche) and Robert Warrior (Osage) describe the importance of the NCAI as "the sole intertribal rallying point from which Indians could engage Congress and the federal bureaucracy on an ongoing basis" (Smith and Warrior 1996, 43). The NCAI continues to exist in the present day, describing itself as "the oldest, largest and most representative American Indian and Alaska Native organization serving the broad interests of tribal governments and communities" (www.ncai.org).

The National Indian Youth Council (NIYC) is notable in the timeline of twentieth-century Native political organization as the "first independent Native youth organization" founded in 1961 (Shreve 2011, 106). Major figures in the NIYC include president and executive director Mel Thom (Paiute), as well as cofounder Clyde Warrior (Ponca). Among many endeavors, the NIYC came to national prominence through its activism in support of Pacific Northwest Indian fishing rights, called "fish-ins," in 1964. Shreve highlights these actions as distinguishing the NIYC from the NCAI (Shreve 2011, 119). These fish-ins, preceding the Alcatraz occupation by five years, provide a model through which to understand the influence of Native student activism on Red Power in the years that followed, as well as Indian articulations of civil disobedience during the civil rights era.

The American Indian Movement (AIM) was originally formed in 1968 as a police-watch organization in Minnesota. Founding members include Clyde Bellecourt (White Earth Ojibwa), Dennis Banks (Leech Lake Ojibwa), and Russell Means (Oglala Lakota). AIM came to national prominence following their support of Oglala Lakota protests into the circumstances behind the racially motivated murder of Raymond Yellow Thunder in 1972 (Smith and Warrior 1996, 113–26). While not associated historically with the occupation of Alcatraz, AIM would go on to play a major role in the previously mentioned Trail of Broken Treaties and Wounded Knee II occupation following Alcatraz.

Having reached 1969, we come now to Alcatraz. While space does not permit a full recounting of the historical background behind the occupation, I do wish to briefly state my reading of the circumstances behind it, as informed by scholarship in Native American Studies (Johnson 2008). Some of these explanations will necessarily overlap with previously mentioned political groups, further explaining the historical context of the time and the issues at stake.

While Red Power politics were representative of both urban and rural Native populations and experiences, the location of Alcatraz near an urban Relocation center helped advance those concerns to a national level. American Indians have been living in cities for as long as any other peoples in the United States. In fact, American Indian Studies scholar Jack Forbes argues that "urban life has been a major aspect of American life from ancient times…from about 1600 to 1700 BC until the 1519–1520 C.E. period, the largest cities in the world were often located in the Americas rather than in Asia, Africa, or Europe" (Forbes 2001, 5). In the 1950s and 1960s, the United States government became involved in the urbanization of American Indians through a series of programs, beginning in 1952 and culminating in 1962 with the Employment Assistance Program, that are referred to as "Relocation" or the "Relocation program" (Johnson 2008, 8). Relocation provided federal assistance to Indians who wished to relocate from their home reservations to urban areas. That federal assistance included "vocational training, assistance in finding employment, and other services to adjust to city life" (8). Major relocation cities include Chicago, Los Angeles, New York, and the San Francisco Bay Area.

The vocational training provided by the government was geared toward low-wage work and therefore many relocatees found themselves facing poverty not unlike what they had tried to leave on their reservations. These difficult economic circumstances were often compounded by sense of cultural disconnect with the urban environment. Since federal assistance to relocatees lasted only through the initial stages of moving to the city and finding a job, many Indians were left without support to deal with these issues. Given these circumstances many analyses of the relocation program locates it as part of a continued policy of forced assimilation of the part of the US federal government (Johnson 2008; Fixico 2000; Moisa 2002).

Many American Indians chose to remain in cities despite the dire social conditions they faced, and it is through the efforts of those individuals and communities that urban American Indians continue to thrive in the present moment. Recognizing the need to address the health and welfare of their communities, urban American Indian activists founded friendship houses, survival schools, and cultural centers in cities across the country to meet the needs of Indian relocatees. Many are still in operation today, such as the Friendship House Association of American Indians in San Francisco and the Intertribal Friendship House in

Oakland, California. These urban American Indian social organizations played an important role in facilitating an intertribal sense of identity, an identity that became progressively more politicized during the 1960s. The occupation of Alcatraz represents a moment in that transformation of consciousness chronicled in the aforementioned timeline. A group called Indians of All Tribes conducted the occupation of the former federal penitentiary of Alcatraz Island on November 20, 1969. The central figures in the organization were students from San Francisco State University, UCLA, and UC Berkeley, including Richard Oakes (Mohawk) and LaNada Warjack (Shoshone Bannock). The group occupied Alcatraz in order to secure a number of demands revolving around the redevelopment of the island in order to meet the needs of local Indian community members. Those demands included federal funds with which to build a cultural center and a university on the island. Indians of All Tribes claimed Alcatraz under the 1868 Treaty of Fort Laramie, which stated that Indians had the right to reclaim unused federal property that had originally been Indian land. The occupation continued under different leaders until June 11, 1971, when the remaining occupiers were removed by the US government. The actions of the occupiers led to greater public awareness of American Indians on reservations and in urban centers. The occupation is commemorated every fall during sunrise ceremonies marking Indigenous Peoples Day (Columbus Day) and Thanksgiving.

NATIVE AMERICAN POPULAR
MUSICIANS OF THE 1960s AND 1970s

Peter La Farge
Peter La Farge (Narragansett, 1931–1965) grew up in Colorado. The adopted son of Oliver La Farge, anthropologist and author of *Laughing Boy* (1930), Peter's early life centered on his activities as a rodeo rider, singer, and songwriter. He served in the Navy during the 1940s in Korea and was awarded five Battle Stars. After completing his Navy service La Farge attended theater school in Chicago and then moved to New York City where he became part of the Greenwich Village folk scene alongside musicians such as Bob Dylan, Pete Seeger, and First Nations folksinger Buffy Sainte-Marie. La Farge recorded five albums on the Folkways label between 1962 and 1965 (Wright-McLeod 2005, 119).

"Custer" (Ping playlist track 2), recorded in 1963, makes use of historical citation to sound activism, providing an American Indian point of view on Lieutenant Colonel George Armstrong Custer and the Battle of Little Bighorn. Custer began his military service in the Union Army, where he eventually ascended to the rank of general. He returned to public life for a short period at the conclusion of the Civil War before joining the newly formed 7th Cavalry at the rank of Lieutenant Colonel. Custer became known as an "Indian fighter" in the late 1860s leading to his participation in the Battle of Little Bighorn in June 1876.

The Battle of Little Bighorn was precipitated by the continuing westward expansion of settlers into Indian Territory in violation of previously guaranteed treaty rights. In the case of Little Bighorn, Lakota, Cheyenne, and Arapaho and other Plains tribes were being forced to relocate to reservations in contradiction of the Treaty of Fort Laramie (1868). Of special concern to Plains tribes was US interest in the Black Hills, a sacred site that the government wished to exploit for the purposes of gold mining.

At the time the battle took place, a number of bands met near the Little Bighorn River in what is now Crow Agency, Montana, to discuss a response to US incursions. As those Natives participating in the gathering assembled in violation of a government order requiring them to return to South Dakota, they were considered hostiles by the military. Members of the 7th Cavalry, including Custer, were dispatched to bring the so-called hostiles to their reservation and clear the way for continued westward expansion. Custer came upon the Indians assembled at Little Bighorn and decided to engage them. The particulars of that engagement have been covered in detail in other sources and I encourage interested readers to seek out those books in order to learn more about this moment in American history (for example, Hardorff 2004). In short, a Native force that included Sitting Bull, Gall, Crazy Horse, and American Horse, defeated Custer and his men and killed Custer in the process.

In this light, La Farge's use of historical citation by quoting a victorious moment in the history of Native resistance to oppression may be heard as sounding activism and allying his performance with social movements of the time. This historical citation accomplishes unique "work" on a number of different levels. On a tribal-specific level, the song recounts the history of the battle and of Custer as he interacted with the Lakota, Cheyenne, and other Native tribes who participated in the event. On another level, listeners from other tribes and listeners who may not even be Indian also experience a new perspective on Custer. Historical citation in this case sounds activism that resonates on both tribal-specific and pan-Indian levels; "Custer's" performance speaks to the ability of soundings to engender new listening communities. In the same way that Native American activists occupied Alcatraz Island, performers and listeners could also be said to participate in occupying the soundscape of the time period by creating and circulating soundings like "Custer."

La Farge's voice, which in this recording straddles the line between speech and song, makes it possible for a listener to follow along with the lyrics and to experience the song as La Farge performs it. This would certainly be in keeping with folk music practice in terms of facilitating the learning and subsequent performance of the song in different versions and by different musicians. The original LP release of "Custer" included a **chord** chart and lyrics and, in keeping with the aesthetic of folk performers such as Pete Seeger, the line between performance and activism becomes blurred through the sharing of such materials making and in fact encouraging repetition and variation.

ACTIVITY 4.2 *Tap along with the pulse of the guitar part on Ping playlist track 2 in order to feel the relationship between the guitar part and La Farge's vocal part.*

Buffy Sainte-Marie

Buffy Sainte-Marie (Figure 4.1) was born on the Piapot Reserve in Saskatchewan, Canada, and was adopted as an infant by a family of Mi'kmaq ancestry. Raised in Massachusetts and Maine, she played piano at an early age and later took up guitar and songwriting as a teenager. She began her musical career performing in coffeehouses while attending the University of Massachusetts, Amherst. She graduated in 1963 with degrees in Oriental philosophy and education, and traveled to New York where she became part of the Greenwich Village folk scene alongside Peter La Farge, Bob Dylan, and others. Sainte-Marie's New York performances in the early 1960s led to her signing with Vanguard Records and the release of her first album, *It's My Way* (1964). The album leads off with "Now that the Buffalo's Gone" (Ping playlist track 3), a song that foreshadows Sainte-Marie's long career of highlighting First Nations and Native American issues through music that continues in the present moment with her most recent release, *Running for the Drum* (2009).

FIGURE 4.1 *Buffy Sainte-Marie, Down East Music Festival, Homer, Alaska, 2012.* Photo by Heidi Aklaseaq Senungetuk, courtesy of Heidi Aklaseaq Senungetuk.

ACTIVITY 4.3 *Listen to Ping playlist track 3 and transcribe Sainte-Marie's lyrics. Check your transcription against that of a classmate or friend.*

"Now that the Buffalo's Gone" is similar to La Farge's "Custer" in that it makes use of historical citation to sound Native issues relevant to the time in which it was recorded. Where La Farge looked from 1963 back to 1867 in sounding "Custer," Sainte-Marie sings about Kinzua Dam, a more recent happening at the time this song was recorded in 1964. Kinzua Dam is located in the Allegheny National Forest in Pennsylvania, and was constructed to facilitate flood control in the area. However, its construction necessitated the forced relocation of many Seneca families, including descendants of the Seneca leader Cornplanter. Those families fought the dam construction by making recourse to the Treaty of Canandaigua (1794) that guaranteed Native title to the land in question. The decision eventually went in favor of the government, Kinzua Dam was constructed, and the Seneca lands were lost to flood. The loss of land that often features in historical discussions of American Indians is shown to continue at the moment the song was recorded. While "Custer" made use of a victorious moment in Native history, "Now that the Buffalo's Gone" cites a moment of loss through which to illustrate the need to remember the event, as well as the need for continued organization and protest. While the Seneca lands may have been flooded, Sainte-Marie follows La Farge in creating a sonic text where Native narratives may be remembered and made relevant to future generations.

Floyd Red Crow Westerman
Floyd Red Crow Westerman (1936–2007) (Figure 4.2) was born on the Sisseton-Wahpeton Dakota Sioux Reservation. He studied art, speech, and theater at Northern State College in South Dakota before moving to Denver to pursue his musical career as a singer, guitarist, and songwriter. Westerman met Native scholar and activist Vine Deloria while living and performing in Denver, and modeled his first album on Deloria's text *Custer Died for Your Sins* (Deloria 1969). Westerman continued to record and went on to maintain a long career in film and television as an actor. Like Sainte-Marie, Westerman also maintained a politically active profile through organizations such as the American Indian Movement and the International Indian Treaty Council (Wright-McLeod 2005, 205–7).

Deloria's text *Custer Died for Your Sins* is subtitled "an Indian Manifesto" and addresses the state of Indian affairs at that time (1969), ranging from land and spirituality to humor and race relations. It played a crucial role in the formation of American Indian Studies due to Deloria's attention to the complexity of Indian experience and the many intersecting forces that inform the formation of American Indian identity. The book's title is derived from a bumper sticker that was originally circulated by the National Congress of American Indians during Deloria's time as president of the organization. Deloria explained the reference:

> "Originally, the Custer bumper sticker referred to the Sioux Treaty of 1868, signed at Fort Laramie, in which the United States pledged to give free and undisturbed use of the lands claimed by Red Cloud in return for peace. Under the covenants of the Old Testament, breaking a covenant called for a blood sacrifice for atonement. Custer was the blood sacrifice for the United States breaking the Sioux treaty. That, at least originally, was the meaning of the slogan" (1969, 148).

FIGURE 4.2 *(Left to right) John-Carlos Perea, Floyd Red Crow Westerman, and Jacob Perea, Native Contemporary Arts Festival, San Francisco, c.1995.* Photo by Barbara Perea, courtesy of the author.

The slogan can still be seen today on items ranging from bumper stickers to tee shirts and in movies and other forms of popular culture.

Westerman recorded the album *Custer Died for Your Sins* in 1970 for Perception Records. Each of the songs on it, including the single version of "Custer Died for Your Sins," is modeled on a chapter or theme from Deloria's book. The original recording is currently not in the catalog and not available on your Ping playlist. Regardless of that, it is worthy of mention because of its relationship to the theme of sounding activism. Where I have characterized the pervious examples as making use of historical citation, *Custer Died for Your Sins* is notable as an example of collaboration between Native musicians and the emerging Native academic presence that would go on to solidify the importance of American Indian Studies into the present day. In this way music can be seen as critical to the formation and dissemination of American Indian Studies today, making audible the importance of sounding activism and alliances. Given this importance I will speak briefly about the single version of "Custer Died for Your Sins" here (1970).

"Custer Died for Your Sins" fuses genres by featuring elements of folk music (acoustic guitar, harmonica) and country music (pedal steel guitar) in the context of a full band arrangement that includes background vocalists. Where La Farge and Sainte-Marie might be heard as singing "on their own," the multiple vocalists on "Custer Died for Your Sins" fill the space so as to communicate the organized sense of community spoken to through the song lyrics. Custer becomes a primary lyrical focus again, but instead of centering the Battle of Little Bighorn as primary, the song addresses pan-Indian historical memories of loss and survival in the different verses.

By repeating the **chorus**—"Custer Died for your Sins"—Custer becomes symbolic at the macro level of the negative relationship between Natives and the United States. What is different here is that those negative aspects are phrased in such a way so that tribal specificity is deemphasized, allowing listeners to identify with the song in an intertribal fashion. Custer's death is celebrated not simply because it marks the passing of a disliked figure but, referring back to the slogan's biblical origins, the death of Custer provides the impetus with which to create change based on the citation of shared historical memories between communities.

Redbone

Redbone was formed in the late 1960s in Los Angeles by brothers Pat and Lolly Vegas (Yaqui and Shoshone), Tony Bellamy (Yaqui), and Pete DePoe (Cheyenne), all of whom were working as session musicians at that time (Wright-McLeod 2005, 157). Redbone's music is notable for its fusion of funk, soul, and "Louisiana swamp rock" (157). The group was particularly influential on the East LA music scene and elements of low rider culture through their song "Come and Get Your Love" (1974). The group was inducted into the Rock and Roll Hall of Fame in 2002.

Redbone signed with Epic Records and released five albums, including *Potlatch*, their second, in 1970. A potlatch is a Native American ceremony based on gift giving and feasting practiced in the Pacific Northwest and in Alaska. The album includes the song "Alcatraz." The album and song are not available online but, due to its direct reference to the occupation, I will discuss it here.

I have located the soundings of La Farge and Sainte-Marie as utilizing historical citation to ally themselves with Red Power and other social movements taking place at the time of their release. Their songs employ conventions of folk music to create sonic texts articulating Native American perspectives and memory. The shared activity of listening creates communities though the social activity of musicking and these communities then come to intersect with others taking place at the same time. Westerman's sounding shows the influence of La Farge and Sainte-Marie in terms of sounding history and memory. He diverges by emphasizing an intertribal identity reflecting transformations also being articulated in social movements and scholarship of the time. Memory and history are being sounded but that history is less about tribal specificity and more about the power to be had through organizing as a group under American Indianness. Westerman's *Custer Died for Your Sins* is also notable as an example of collaboration between Native musicians and Native academics.

An intertribal consciousness can also be heard in Redbone's "Alcatraz." The song records one perspective on what took place on the island during the period of occupation. It diverges from previous soundings by employing a rock ballad format. Acoustic guitar is heard supplying a rhythmic framework over a bass drum pulse. The inclusion of electric bass guitar and electric guitar played through a rotating Leslie speaker creates associations with rock and roll of the time. The song's lyrics explain the occupation in terms of beauty, explaining that the changes sought by the occupiers are taking place because Indians "care." Throughout the song, an intertribal identity is reinforced by references to "the Indian" rather than to tribal-specific identities. In a fashion similar to Westerman's sounding, the song **refrain** is almost customized for group singing, allowing participants to bond through repetition of the word "Alcatraz." In this way Redbone's "Alcatraz" can be heard as sounding activism through collaboration with the occupiers and occupation, recording it and making it available to larger audiences through performance and on record.

By recording the occupation, Redbone follow the example of the previous artists in terms of creating texts through which memory is maintained. Redbone's example illustrates that memory is not just something that happened in the past. Their sounding of "Alcatraz" allows us to hear one sonic perspective of the soundscape of the island. It should be recognized that this sounding was not limited in its circulation. The first single on *Potlatch*, "Maggie," reached number forty-five on the Billboard pop charts. This number reveals one measurement of Redbone's popularity at the time and would suggest that sales of their music reached larger audiences than might be assumed for a Native American rock band. Regardless of sales, their sounding shows the intersection and collaboration between musical and political circulation and the many ways in which the occupation and the events that followed became part of American consciousness through popular music.

ACTIVITY 4.4   *Go to your local library or used record store and look for copies of Westerman's* Custer Died for Your Sins *and Redbone's* Potlach. *If you do find them, take note of where the recordings are filed at your library or store. Were they labeled as Native American or something else?*

XIT

XIT (pronounced "exit") (Figure 4.3) is a Native rock and roll band formed in 1971 and featuring vocalist guitarist A. Michael Martin (Chicano, Laguna Pueblo), drummer Leeja Herrera (Pueblo), bassist Jomac Suazo (Taos Peublo), and guitarist R. C. Garriss (intertribal Oklahoma Native), and lyricist and manager Tom Bee (Dakota) (Wright-McLeod 2005, 215; Romero 2011, 291). The group began as Lincoln Street Exit in 1968 and transitioned into XIT under the management of Bee, who became known early in his musical career for his songwriting skills. Before XIT, Bee had worked for Motown records with both the Jackson 5 ("We've Got Blue Skies" [1971]) and vocalist Smokey Robinson. Bee's success led to a record deal with a Motown record label subsidiary called Rare Earth Records, under whose imprint XIT recorded *Plight of the Redman* (1972) at Motown's Hitsville Studios in Detroit. The group continues to record and perform today as The Original XIT Boyz.

I describe *Plight of the Redman* to my classes as a concept album because the progression of songs relates a particular story. In this case, the story begins on side A of the album with its descriptions of Native life before the arrival of Columbus. Side B begins with the song "The Coming of the Whiteman" and describes relations up to the present moment. The album concludes with a song called "End?" (Ping playlist track 4), in which the album's content is brought into the present moment by summarizing historical and contemporary issues and events at that time. XIT's recording of "End?" marked a transitional phase in the Red Power movement following the occupation of Alcatraz and looking to other events in which the American Indian Movement would become a prominent organizing force such as the Wounded Knee II occupation.

The song begins with backing vocalists singing a refrain in the Navajo language over pow-wow dance bells and percussion. Ethnomusicologist David McAllester transcribed and translated the opening verses (1981), sung in the Navajo language as *"Hey ya hey / Akodaani / Dii nihi keyah ho / Akonisin"* (This we say, this is our country, this we wish). The repetition

FIGURE 4.3   *XIT, c.1973. (Back row, left to right) Obie Sullivan, Leeja Herrera, Jomac Suazo, R. C. Gariss Jr. (Front row, left to right) Chili Yazzie, Tom Bee, Tyrone King.*   Photo by Alton Walpole, courtesy of Tom Bee, SOAR Records, © 1973 Tom Bee. All rights reserved.

of these phrases forms the rhythmic and melodic foundation for the rest of the component parts of the song, which prominently features a string section as part of the overall arrangement. While other songs on *Plight of the Redman* do feature sung vocals, "End?" features a spoken vocal by A. Michael Martin that uses historical citation to again ally the performance with Red Power as it moved into the 1970s following events such as the occupation of Alcatraz and fish-ins at Fort Lawton, Washington.

ACTIVITY 4.5   *Listen to Ping playlist track 4 and transcribe the speech beginning at 0:38. Check your transcription with a friend or classmate.*

In this chapter you have read about and listened to the ways in which Native American musicians sounded political activism in the 1960s and 1970s by allying themselves with political and social movements. Rather than just assume that musicians are part of a movement because they lived and performed during a particular time period, Diamond's alliance studies model allows us to characterize the actual methods used by performers to link their performances through sound. In the case of the artists covered here, those methods included historical citation, collaboration, and use of language. This way of thinking about music is in keeping with the focus of this text to look at music as a social activity and foregrounds what musicians do with music rather than assuming that music is a thing or object unto itself.

The sounding of activism by Native popular musicians is by no means limited to the 1960s and 1970s. Sainte-Marie continues to perform in the present moment and is known for modifying and updating the lyrics to her songs in order to reflect political issues relevant to her and her audiences. The lens of alliance studies provides insight into later soundings that have become influential to intertribal Native American music such as the collaboration between the Navajo punk rock trio Blackfire and punk icon Joey Ramone on their album *One Nation Under* (2002). The intertribal exchange between Canada and the United States is illuminated again by the collaborations between First Nations hip-hop group War Party and Public Enemy founder Chuck D. on War Party's *The Resistance* (1997). More recently, the First Nations DJ crew A Tribe Called Red created the song "The Road" (2012), featuring their fusion of powwow singing and drumming and electronic dance music (Pow Wow Step) to show support for #IdleNoMore and Attawapiskat Chief Theresa Spence. These examples show the depth of the circuits in which Native American popular musicians travel and make audible the fact that activism, like music, is not simply a thing; it is a social process through which listeners learn not only about Native American musicians and issues but also about themselves.

CHAPTER 5

Sounding Unexpectedness: Native American Jazz Musicians

As you read in the previous chapter, artists such as Buffy Sainte-Marie and Peter La Farge played a formative role in the early stages of the Greenwich Village folk scene, a scene that is recognized for other musical luminaries such as Bob Dylan. The American Indian rock and roll of XIT took shape in the same recording studio as many of the greatest Motown Records hits. These musicians who played Western instruments and often played in "non-Indian" styles are often overlooked because they do not sound Indian in an "expected" fashion. In this chapter I expand upon previous research (Perea 2009; 2012) to further explore the idea of what constitutes intertribal Native American music in the United States through the subject of Native jazz musicians, including Mildred Bailey (Coeur d'Alene), Russell "Big Chief" Moore (Akimel O'odham [Pima], Oscar Pettiford (Choctaw, Cherokee), and Jim Pepper (Creek, Kaw). Their "unexpected" presence in the genre of jazz complicates the idea of what constitutes American and American Indian musics.

My use of the term "unexpected" in this chapter is derived from the work of cultural historian Philip J. Deloria (Dakota) in his text *Indians in Unexpected Places* (2004). He argues that cultural expectations of American Indians as primitive, technologically incompetent, and distant "are both the products and the tools of domination...an inheritance that haunts each and every one of us" (Deloria 2004, 4). I agree with Deloria that it is crucial to question and explore expectations of American Indians because "they created—and they continue to reproduce—social, political, legal, and economic relations that are asymmetrical, sometimes grossly so" (2004, 4). Deloria examines the lives of Native Americans who participated in forms of culture—film, music, athletics, and others—where American Indians were not expected to be found in the late nineteenth and early twentieth centuries by virtue of their supposed distance and primitivism. Rather than view these individuals as anomalous in relation to stereotyped expectations—a move that reinforces the power of expectations in the first place—Deloria locates Native American presence in the aforementioned genres of American popular culture as "unexpected," a source of agency and power through which expectation is questioned and refuted to reveal a much more complex picture of Native American and American lives. Following the work of musicologist and jazz pianist David Ake (2002, 14), I want to make audible the "cultural transgressions, tensions, and contradictions—as well as new senses of kinship" that can come from making the unexpected sound of Native jazz musicians audible within the history of a musical form Natives are not commonly associated with in American popular culture.

A BRIEF DETOUR THROUGH
RHYTHM ON THE RESERVATION

In my Introduction to American Indian Studies course at San Francisco State University, I use different media examples drawn from movies, commercials, and cartoons from different periods in time in order to introduce students to the concept of expectations as a way of asking them to think about the many factors that influence American Indian identity. In the process of updating my library of clips, my teaching assistant, Cassandra Freeman (Odawa, Sioux), introduced me to a Betty Boop cartoon called *Rhythm on the Reservation* (1938) that is relevant both to understanding expectations and also to Native jazz musicians and sounding unexpectedness. I will describe the cartoon below to set the stage for the discussion to follow.

Before proceeding, I want to acknowledge that the discussion of stereotyping and expectation is extremely difficult, complex, and personal. I do not, however, view those qualities as negative. As I wrote in chapter 1, when I ask my students to brainstorm the many terms used in popular culture to refer to Native Americans, I ask them to list stereotypical terms along with more acceptable or "polite" terms because the violence embedded in words like "redskin" and "squaw" is still very present today and should not be overlooked. By speaking these terms a space is created in which they can be discussed and through that process students may come to their own personally relevant understandings of why such language is disrespectful.

Where discussions of naming terminology focus on language and representation, *Rhythm on the Reservation* adds visual and musical representation to the conversation. The analysis and discussion of cartoons are relevant to both music and Native American studies. Daniel Goldmark's *Tunes for 'Toons: Music and the Hollywood Cartoon* examines among other subjects cartoon music and stereotyping in relation to race and gender, noting that "stereotypes played specifically to cultural expectations of appearance and sound" (2005, 30). Filmmaker Neil Diamond (Cree) also examines expectations of appearance and sound in *Reel Injun: On the Trail of the Hollywood Indian* (2009), making use of examples from cinema, television, and multiple cartoons. In this case, I want to pay attention to expectations of appearance and sound in *Rhythm on the Reservation* and how Native jazz musicians active from the 1930s onward did not reproduce the expectations articulated in the cartoon. It should also be noted that while I am interpreting a Betty Boop cartoon, the focus is on Native American representations and not on the image of Betty. While beyond the scope of the present chapter, a discussion of Betty Boop as a problematic female cartoon character in her own right is worthy of a separate discussion on representations of women and femininity in media over time.

Betty Boop was the creation of the Fleischer cartoon studio in 1930. *Rhythm on the Reservation* was made in 1939 toward the end of Betty Boop's run as a cartoon character. In this short, Betty is first seen driving a car with a large sign proclaiming "Betty Boop's Swing Band." To reinforce the sign the car is loaded down with a number of instruments, including an acoustic bass, a drum set, a harp, and a trumpet. Betty stops the car and proclaims: "Oh gee, real Indians!" The perspective shifts to reveal that Betty has driven up to the "Wigwam Beauty Shop," whose sign asks passerby to "Try Our Scalp Treatment," a reference to the act of scalping.

An Indian woman of indeterminate tribal origin observes Betty looking at the sign and turns to attract the attention of her male counterpart. The Indian male is sleeping underneath a tree and snoring in an exaggerated fashion. The woman throws an object at the male to wake him up. The male wakes and walks over to the woman who says: "Ug customer makeum ballyhoo!" The woman hands the man a drum that he plays by hanging it around his neck like a marching bass drum. Betty hears the sound and walks over to the pair.

Betty approaches the man and woman and says: "Oh, how do you do Mr. Redskin? I'd like to buy a tom-tom." The Indian man offers her a bracelet and Betty refuses. He offers her moccasins and Betty refuses again, pointing to the drum around the man's neck and saying: "No, I want tom-tom." The man looks at his female companion, who during the exchange has sat near the two, staring dourly off into the distance, removes the drum from around his neck, and says: "Me giveum tomtom." Betty thanks the Indian man while the Indian woman casts scathing glances in his direction.

Perspective shifts again and we are taken back to Betty's car filled with musical instruments. A group of Indians has now surrounded the car and through gesture and grunting appear to be trying to make sense of the vehicle and its contents. Meanwhile, back at the Wigwam Beauty Shop, the Indian woman has had enough. She jumps up and with an angry "ug!" takes the tom-tom from Betty's hands. She shoves the drum roughly into the Native man's chest while Betty protests: "I wanted to buy that!" Another perspective shift and we see that the Indians surrounding Betty's car have overcome their fears and are taking the musical instruments away for themselves. Betty returns to the car in distress at finding her instruments taken. It is at this point in the cartoon where I wish to focus on the visual deployment of a particular set of musical expectations regarding American Indians.

Following Betty's discovery of the missing instruments, the viewer is shown various scenes of Native Americans trying to make sense of the band instruments they took from Betty's car. A Native man tries to play a trombone but instead uses it to pump water from a small lake, saying "Makeum spring!" These actions are a source of laughter for Betty who says "Look at the fun they're having, aren't they cute?" A series of images follows: A Native man using a violin and bow to start a fire and cook food, a Native man using an accordion as a bellows to keep a fire going, a Native man using a hi-hat cymbal to flatten out arrowheads, a Native boy using an acoustic bass case as a canoe. These are all sight gags, visual jokes based on musical expectations of American Indians. The assumption would appear to be that Native Americans had no knowledge of these instruments and therefore could not be expected to play them as others might. The humor comes therefore from taking a musical instrument and using it for a purpose for which it is not intended.

Betty, now standing in her empty car, laughs at the young boy in the bass case canoe, "Isn't he a little darling?" The Indian man from the opening scenes climbs into the car next to her and makes cartoonish sexual overtures, "Hello Toots!" The two laugh together at the boy and the bass case canoe before the Indian woman from the opening scene, whom we might now think of as the man's wife or companion, stands before the car with a club or tomahawk in her hands. The Indian man, caught in the act of flirting with Betty, runs off screen with his wife/companion in pursuit. Betty exclaims "I wonder what's a matter with her?" before turning back to observe the Indians and her stolen musical instruments.

A Native man tries to light a fire under a timpanum drum and use it as a cooking vessel. Betty walks over to him and says, "That's no pot, that's tom-tom." The man repeats "Tom-tom?" as if to question Betty's explanation. She then proceeds to play the tympani with a galloping duple beat that the Indian in the shot joins in playing. The sound of this new beat attracts the rest of the camp and we see more shots of instruments being used out of context. Interestingly enough, the tasks shown also have a gendered dimension. Where the Indian men were using instruments to pump water or make arrowheads, Indian women are showing using a xylophone to wash clothes and percussion mallets to pound grain.

A musical number begins where Betty teaches the Natives in the camp to properly play the musical instruments and to "play the swing she craves." A series of visual jokes, continuing to show Indians misusing musical instruments, is developed around the musical number. I would qualify the music and the dance shown as referencing big band swing music. Music historian Daniel Goldmark recognizes Fleischer Studios for their use of jazz in the 1920s and 1930s "in that they treated it not as background but as a musical genre deserving of recognition" (2005, 84). In fact, a wide variety of jazz musicians active during that time period featured in Fleischer cartoons including, among others, Cab Calloway and Louis Armstrong (2005). Goldmark also analyzes the creation of expectations relating to jazz and African American jazz musicians in these cartoons, noting the manner in which Fleischer and Warner Bros. studios emphasized the primitiveness of jazz's origins and the racialization of African American jazz musicians (2005, 84–92).

Viewing the cartoon in this light, if jazz is a primitive music form then Native Americans are apparently even more primitive as they cannot understand the instruments or play the swing music Betty wants unless she teaches it to the camp. Even with Betty teaching the camp through her song, the animated Natives continue to misuse the instruments, reinforcing the perception that Natives are too ignorant to understand a musical form already contextualized in previous cartoons as primitive itself. The musical number concludes once again with the Native man from the opening sequence dancing suggestively with Betty Boop. He dances her back into her car and she drives away, "Goodbye Mr. Redskin!" The Native man is shown riding behind

Betty's car on a blanket in an attempt to leave the camp and perhaps follow Betty to her next stop. He is lassoed from out of frame, though, and falls backward to land at the feet of his angry female companion. She beats the man to the rhythm of a swing drum break and the cartoon fades to the end.

There are any number of different ways to view and to analyze Betty Boop and the Native Americans she meets in *Rhythm on the Reservation*. Here I am most concerned with the expectation articulated in the cartoon that Native Americans would have had no idea what to with Westernized musical instruments in 1939 and that Native Americans were too primitive to even comprehend jazz. Recent scholarship in ethnomusicology and Native American Studies outlines the historical factors and lived experiences that make audible the unexpected contributions of Native American musicians to the field of jazz.

UNEXPECTED ORIGIN STORIES: NATIVE AMERICAN MUSICIANS IN THE BOARDING SCHOOL SYSTEM

Lieutenant Richard Henry Pratt founded the Carlisle Indian Industrial School in 1879. Pratt came to prominence first during the Civil War and later in his career as a commander of Indian scouts (Prucha 1986, 235). As part of his military service Pratt began to develop an educational philosophy as well as various programs to teach his philosophy, which were tested on Indian prisoners of war under his command. His work gathered support until its culmination in the founding of the Indian Industrial School at Carlisle, Pennsylvania. Pratt's educational agenda may be understood as emphasizing forced assimilation as central to Native educational success: "He insisted upon complete integration of the Indians into white society, and his whole program was geared to that goal" (1986, 235). This philosophy has led Pratt and the Carlisle Indian Industrial School to become most often associated with instances of physical and mental abuse—such as forbidding the students to speak their tribal language or forcibly cutting their hair—that took place at Carlisle as well as at other boarding schools during this period in American history.

Historian John W. Troutman has written about the ways in which music was used in the boarding school context as part of that assimilationist educational agenda shared by Pratt and the United States government: "While primarily the girls were trained in domestic labor and the boys were trained in industrial labor, the students' 'transformation' also required, according to the OIA [Office of Indian Affairs], training in the 'proper arts of civilization'…musical education was absolutely fundamental to Pratt's purpose" (2009, 112–13). The purpose of this musical education was to provide Native students attending boarding schools such as Carlisle with a non-Indian cultural alternative to their own tribal music culture. This introduction to the music superculture was viewed as facilitating the students' ability to better and faster assimilate into the role of an American rather than remain a member of a specific tribe or nation (113–14). Pratt felt that these types of performance opportunities provided to Native students "the discipline, refinement, and cultural attributes necessary from them to eventually become proper American citizens" (118).

Recent scholarship in Native American musical history has resituated aspects of the boarding school experience to recognize both disappearance and survivance. While many lost their lives or aspects of their identities, the histories of those who survived also play an important role in understanding what it means to be Indian over time. Troutman cites the example of Lakota coronetist Luther Standing Bear, who led the Carlisle band across the Brooklyn Bridge during its opening ceremonies in 1883 (Troutman 2009, 138–9). While Deloria is primarily concerned with the late 1800s and early 1900s, Troutman and Janis Johnson extend their analyses of Native American musical history to look at the formation of Native American bands beyond the school context by former boarding school students and the status achieved by those musicians on their respective circuits (Troutman 2009, 201–252; Johnson 2010, 197–221).

When I observe the timeline assembled by Deloria, Troutman, and Johnson I am reminded both of the historical legacy of forced Native American educational and cultural assimilation and the new ways found by Native American musicians to perform their own personal sense of Indianness. By sounding their unexpectedness, whether it was marching across the Brooklyn Bridge or—as you will see—rearranging **peyote** songs to include jazz, rock, and country influences, Deloria's, Troutman's, and Johnson's analyses make audible the fact that Native American musicians did not simply assimilate, as was expected at that time in American history. Instead, I hear these musicians through Deloria's analysis as sounding unexpectedness through performances and lived experiences that critique the idea of Native disappearance and assimilation in the first place (Deloria 2004, 11).

NATIVE AMERICAN JAZZ MUSICIANS

Rhythm on the Reservation can now be revisited with the understanding that Native Americans had, for sixty years before the creation of that cartoon, been active participants in Westernized musical education, through boarding schools and other similar entities, performing in many styles including jazz. I will now examine a selected group of Native American jazz musicians who have come to be recognized in the contemporary discussion to highlight Native American influences in jazz. Although some of these individuals did not attend a boarding school, I hear them as linked to *Rhythm on the Reservation* and the boarding schools through the common theme of jazz performance and instrumentation.

Mildred Bailey

Vocalist Mildred Elanor [Rinker] Bailey (Coeur d'Alene, Irish, 1903–1951) was born in Tekoa, Washington. Music journalist and radio producer Brian Wright-McLeod writes that Bailey's mother inspired her daughter to take up singing via trips to her home reservation. The family eventually moved to Spokane, Washington, where Bailey and her brother, vocalist Al Rinker (1907–1982), met and began working with a young Bing Crosby. Bailey began working professionally as a musician at the age of sixteen in Spokane and soon traveled to Los Angeles to continue her professional career in the early 1920s (Wright-McLeod 2005, 50–53).

Bailey, her brother Al Rinker, and Bing Crosby continued their association after moving to Los Angeles. Those circuits brought Bailey into contact with swing bandleader Paul Whiteman who, after being introduced to Bailey through Rinker and Crosby in 1929, hired the singer to perform with his band. Her recording career in the 1930s includes appearances with Whiteman and Benny Goodman. During the 1930s she also recorded what has become one of her signature songs, "Rockin' Chair" (Ping playlist track 5), written by Hoagy Carmichael. The song features a rich musical arrangement based upon a duple rhythm, or two feel, played on guitar. On top of that rhythm you can hear a saxophone section providing background statements to Bailey's vocal. Later in the excerpt a muted brass section enters to add another layer of counterpoint and **texture** to the arrangement. Bailey's voice features prominently over all, displaying a timbre and sense of phrasing that may be heard as in line with the lineage of blues and jazz queens of the early twentieth century. Keep in mind that this song was recorded one to two years before *Rhythm on the Reservation* was made.

ACTIVITY 5.1 *Listen at least five times through to Ping play-list track 5, for each of the musical elements mentioned in the previous paragraph. Transcribe the song's lyrics, circling any empha-sized words or phrases. How do the lyrics and musical arrangement work together to create the feeling of a rocking chair?*

Bailey expanded her career to radio, hosting programs in both the United States and Canada. She was diagnosed with diabetes in 1949 and passed on in 1951. Although Bailey did not attend a boarding school, her participation at the time in the emerging Pacific Northwest jazz scene and her influence on national and international circuits of jazz refute the expectation of Native American assimilation brought about through the boarding school influence. Bailey's life and music have been newly revitalized in the present day through the performances of jazz vocalist Julia Keefe (Nez Perce). Tim Johnson (Mohawk), assistant director for museum programs at the National Museum of the American Indian in Washington, DC, recognized Keefe both for her performances of Bailey's repertoire and her advocacy for the recognition of Bailey's importance to jazz history. The Idaho senate passed a formal resolution honoring Bailey in 2012.

Russell "Big Chief" Moore
Trombonist Russell Moore (Akimel O'odham [Pima], 1912–1983) was born in Bapchule, Arizona, and raised at Gila Crossing in the Gila River Indian Community (Wright-McLeod 2005, 140–42). After his father died early in Moore's life, he was sent to live in Illinois with an uncle who worked as a music teacher and who introduced Russell to brass instruments. Moore began studies of trombone, his main instrument, while a student at the Sherman Institute, a residential boarding school located in Riverside, California. Following boarding school, Moore's career includes, among many others, appearances as a member of Lionel Hampton's big band in the 1930s and Louis Armstrong's Big Band and Sextet in the 1940s. Moore continued to add to his prodigious perfor-mance résumé in the 1950s with a tour of Europe and by recording with clarinetist and saxophonist Sidney Bechet. The trombonist rejoined Armstrong in the 1960s as a member of the trumpeter's All-Star Band.

Moore is featured alongside Armstrong in a television appearance on "The Bell Telephone Hour" from 1965. The performance features a sextet of trumpet and vocal, clarinet, trombone, bass, piano, and drums performing "Basin Street Blues," one of Armstrong's signature songs. Moore can be seen standing to Armstrong's right throughout. The interaction between the trumpet, trombone, and clarinet in the opening of the song recalls the Dixieland sounds with which Armstrong is most often associated in American music history and over the course of his career. Armstrong sings the first verse, which concludes with a drum fill accelerating the song to double time or twice the speed of its opening tempo. Clarinet and acoustic bass solos are featured before Moore takes center stage with a trombone solo. Moore makes use of a plunger mute to employ different timbres, continuously changing the sound of the trombone throughout and adding a vocal quality to his phrasing. Armstrong reenters and Moore discards the mute, returning to his original unmuted sound. Armstrong solos to a full band accompaniment that ends with another drum fill and a closing cadence at the double time tempo.

"I Still Get Jealous," from the 1940s musical *High Button Shoes* (Ping playlist track 6), provides another opportunity to hear Moore in the context of his performances with Armstrong. The group features the same **instrumentation** as the video clip with the addition of banjo. Moore's trombone is featured in a **polyphonic** setting similar to "Basin Street Blues," involving dialogue between trombone, voice, muted trumpet, and clarinet.

ACTIVITY 5.2   *After listening to Ping playlist track 6, do an Internet search on Louis Armstrong. Answer the following questions: Who was Louis Armstrong? Why is he considered important to the history of jazz in the United States? Do your expectations of jazz music change after learning about Russell Moore and hearing him play with Louis Armstrong?*

Moore continued to perform, tour internationally, and record up until the time of his death in 1983. Moore's life and history continue to be revitalized in the present moment through the Russell Moore Music Festival on the Gila River Reservation in Arizona and through museum exhibits such as the Arizona Musical Instrument Museum's "I am AZ Music" (2012) and the National Museum of the American Indian's "Up Where We Belong" (2012).

Oscar Pettiford

Bassist Oscar Pettiford (Choctaw, Cherokee, 1922–1960) (Figure 5.1) was born in Okmulgee, Oklahoma, and raised in Mississippi (Wright-McLeod 2005, 152–4). He began his musical career on bass performing with the family band led by his father, Doc Pettiford and his Family Orchestra, in Minnesota. He left his family band after his father passed on, and after a move from Minneapolis to New York in 1944, Pettiford met and joined the band of bop pioneer Dizzy Gillespie. The bassist's

FIGURE 5.1   *Oscar Pettiford*, The New Oscar Pettiford Sextet, *1999.*   *Courtesy of Concord Music Group.*

performances in the groundbreaking context of bebop would lead to appearances with, among others, Duke Ellington, Thelonious Monk, and Stan Getz. Pettiford died in Denmark in 1960. Many of his compositions, such as "Midnight at Bohemia," have become jazz standards, iconic compositions in the collected repertoire of jazz musicians looked at both as teaching tools and vital performance repertoire.

In addition to his role as a sideman, Pettiford was recognized for his formidable acoustic bass and cello technique. He recorded extensively, leading his ensembles as the main melody instrument, a role that was not normally assigned to the upright bass in the early history of recorded music. Pettiford was able to fulfill the role due to his ability to produce a singing, penetrating tone and fluid phrasing. Pettiford performs Billy Strayhorn's "Stardust" on Ping playlist track 7.

In Pettiford's version of "Stardust" he is accompanied only by piano. The liberal phrasing of the song, with Pettiford embellishing every phrase in a very active manner, would indicate that the bassist and pianist were paying very close attention to each other in the studio in order to move the song forward. Due to Pettiford's technical dexterity and sure knowledge of the song's melody, the line between soloing and playing the melody here is deeply blurred. One could hear the solo more in the manner of a saxophonist or other wind instrument **improvising** on a melody, making reference to the song but always embellishing so as to give the listener a reference, while also encouraging them to keep listening. As a bassist myself, I find it most interesting that Pettiford simultaneously fulfills the basic role of the bass—keeping the song moving—while embellishing the melody in the manner of a wind player. It is that technique that to this day finds Oscar Pettiford referred to as one of the great jazz bassists of all time.

ACTIVITY 5.3 *Search on iTunes for a recording of Louis Armstrong playing "Stardust" on trumpet. Compare and contrast the two performances, taking into account that Armstrong is playing trumpet and Pettiford is playing bass.*

Jim Pepper
Saxophonist and vocalist Jim Pepper (Creek, Kaw, 1941–1992) (Figure 5.2) was born in Portland, Oregon. As a child, Pepper was influenced

FIGURE 5.2   *Ron Thorne (drums), Jim Pepper (saxophone), "Spirit Days," June 19, 1987, Anchorage, Alaska.*   Photo by Patti Thorne, from the collection of Ron and Patti Thorne.

by a wide range of music including tap dance, big band jazz, pow-wow singing, fancy dance, and peyote music. He moved to New York in the early 1960s to join The Free Spirits, with guitarist Larry Coryell and drummer Bob Moses, and later went on to join Everything Is Everything with former Free Spirits bassist Chris Hills. Their eponymous debut release (1969) featured the song "Witchi Tai To," an original arrangement by Pepper of a peyote song learned from his paternal grandfather (Perea 2012, 73).

Pepper explained that "Witchi Tai To" is "a Comanche peyote song, one of many peyote songs that are sung at the time when water is passed around at a peyote meeting" (Smith 1988, 155–6). Pepper's "Witchi Tai To" charted for five weeks on the Billboard pop charts between February 8 and March 8, 1969, peaking at number 69. The song was rerecorded by Pepper on his subsequent albums as a leader following its initial release with Everything is Everything and was also covered by over seventy artists in genres ranging from folk and jazz to electronic music. After releasing four albums as a leader and working with a number of internationally recognized jazz figures, including trumpeter Don Cherry and pianist Mal Waldron, Pepper passed away on February 10, 1992, in Portland, Oregon (Perea 2012, 74).

You have two versions of "Witchi Tai To" on your Ping playlist, one from Pepper's fourth album, The Path, labeled "Witchi Tia To" (Ping playlist track 8), and the other from a 2006 rerelease of one of Pepper's final shows from 1991 (Ping playlist track 9). The original 1969 recording is not available online and so it is not referenced in the following description and activity. Ping playlist track 8 is an example of a jazz arrangement of "Witchi Tai To," featuring Pepper on tenor sax soloing over rhythmic piano accompaniment. Pepper's voice enters in the last ten seconds, singing the lyrics to "Witchi Tai To." Ping playlist track 9 is taken from the introduction to a longer live version of "Witchi Tai To." While "Witchi Tai To" is not performed in the short example available online, the example is still relevant as far as illustrating Pepper singing in a modified peyote style. Pepper begins by singing in English with a turtle rattle accompaniment. The song, "You must not forget me," sounds to my ears like a pow-wow round dance song that Pepper has rearranged in the moment as part of the longer song introduction. At 0:38 Pepper increases the tempo and begins to sing in a modified peyote style. I use the qualifier in this case because Pepper is performing with a rattle but without the water drum accompaniment that is common to peyote singing. Pepper moves back and forth between singing in an unidentified Native language, vocables, and back to English, in which he quotes from the Navajo Beauty Way ceremony and prayer before the excerpt fades out.

ACTIVITY 5.4 *Compare Ping playlist track 8 to the other examples by Bailey, Moore, and Pettiford. Make a list of the ways in which Pepper's jazz is similar to or different than the other jazz artists discussed in this chapter. Think in terms of instrumentation, vocal quality, and rhythmic feel.*

THINKING ABOUT UNEXPECTEDNESS

In this chapter I have introduced the concept of sounding unexpectedness as a way through which to listen to intertribal Native American music as challenging expectations derived from American historical narratives. While the study of expectation is potentially limitless, I chose to focus on American Indian musical expectations through reference to early cartoons. The expectations of American Indian musical primitiveness and the inability to play or comprehend jazz are false but the magnitude of this falseness comes into view through an understanding of the federal boarding school system in the United States. Music was used as part of an overall program of forced assimilation whose cultural trauma is still being felt and dealt with today by organizations such as the Truth and Reconciliation Commission in Canada and the Boarding School Healing Project in the United States. In this way, the representations in *Rhythm on the Reservation* are not simply disrespectful because they are cartoonish; they are disrespectful because they omit the history in favor of telling one side of the story and creating stereotyped expectations based on that single story.

This is the value of unexpectedness, as it provides a frame through which to see the ways that performers and music can be heard as challenging such narratives. The expectation that Native Americans do not play jazz is called into question by the long history of Native involvement in the genre that extends far beyond the four musicians profiled here. The influence of Jim Pepper was incredibly important to my own musical career because it gave me not just a sense of presence in the field of jazz but a historical precedent of Native American involvement through which to locate myself. Saxophonist and poet Joy Harjo points out the long history of Native and African involvement in the Southeastern United States and the implications for that history in shaping new understandings of jazz (2002, 224). Such continued research can only continue to broaden our shared understanding of what constitutes "America's classical music."

CHAPTER 6

Epilogue: The 2012 GRAMMY®
Category Restructuring and Future
Definitions of Intertribal Native
American Music

In this book I have tried to avoid hard-and-fast distinctions between historical and contemporary genres of intertribal Native American music. The origin stories of pow-wow music may locate it in early Native American ceremonial societies but a song like Northern Cree's "Facebook Drama" shows that pow-wow music is simultaneously historical and contemporary music. To hold pow-wow music to one standard or another diminishes the influence of the performers and their performances. I hear Native American flute music in a similar fashion: the idea is not that a choice need be made between American Indian or tribal-specific and Native American or globalized concepts of flute playing, but that listeners understand that both are essential to the health of the genre as it continues to circulate at local, national, and international levels. The activism sounded by Native American popular musicians and the unexpectedness sounded by Native jazz musicians introduced here was sounded between forty to seventy-five years ago. However, rather than think of those soundings as old or historical recordings, I suggest that the resounding of those recordings in the present moment brings those musicians and performances into the present moment, where they can be cited or not in relation to changing generational perspectives influences. In this way, one of the foundational lessons to be learned from the many histories of intertribal Native American music is that it has always been traditional for Native American musicians to be contemporary.

One marker of that contemporary influence and presence that was also very influential on my own career as a musician was the institution of a Best Native American Album category and Grammy award by the Recording Academy in 2001. The mission statement of the Recording Academy is "to positively impact the lives of musicians, industry members and our society at large" (http://www.grammy.org/recording-academy). That statement is engaged at local and national levels through a number of endeavors, ranging from performance rights, education, and health initiatives to what is perhaps their most publicly visible event, the yearly Grammy award ceremony and telecast. The Grammy awards are decided by the voting membership of the Recording Academy and as such are a form of national peer recognition.

The potential social and economic implications of that recognition for performers and musical scenes is immense and so I remember the personal sense of pride and, more importantly, of presence I felt in 2001 when the Best Native American Album category was announced. In a 2001 *New York Times* article, author Neil Strauss characterized the process leading up to the institution of the category both in terms of Native American music industry advocacy and of recognizing the popularity of Native American artists on a national stage and in a variety of musical genres and media forms (Strauss 2001). Sound of America (SOAR) record label owner and XIT member Tom Bee was quoted at the time as saying "it's like landing an Indian on the moon. Do you realize how proud Native Americans watching the Grammys all over the country are going to be when they see that? It's going to inspire so many more musicians to come forth" (2001). I was one of the musicians who "came forth" during that time period and watched the Grammy awards in order to track both nominees and winners and to experience the musi-cultural shifts that came through the awards. Those shifts included Verdell Primeaux (Dakota, Ponca) and Johnny Mike's (Navajo) 2002 Grammy for *Bless the People: Harmonized Peyote Songs* (2002), recognizing peyote singing, and Mary Youngblood's two Grammy awards in 2003 and 2007, mentioned in chapter 3, recognizing changes in Native American flute performance culture with regard to women's and men's roles.

These changes and new visibility were also accompanied by controversy. While attention was paid in the formulation of the category to make sure that musicians and genres were being placed into competition on a fair, genre-to-genre basis, this led to a binary distinction between "traditional" and contemporary genres of Native American music. As described by R. Carlos Nakai in 2002, the Best Native American Album award became problematic over time as "another example...of stereotyping us and saying that the only qualifiable music for an award is traditional American Indian music either in chant or in group-chant form with a drum" (Nakai, as quoted in Brockman 2002).

This situation changed dramatically in April 2011 when the Recording Academy restructured the 2012 Grammy award categories. In that process, the Best Native American Album category and award were discontinued and combined, along with Best Hawaiian, Best Cajun/ Zydeco, and Best Polka into the Regional Roots category. These decisions were based upon internal review by the Recording Academy, oriented towards ensuring the continued competitiveness and related prestige of the Grammy awards (http://www.grammy.org/recording-academy/ announcement/press-release). The restructuring was met with a number of reactions from within the Native American music industry that continue to reflect and articulate a tension between historical and contemporary genres of Native American music and how those can both be equitably represented through an awards process like the Grammys (for example, see Schulman 2011 for a range of views).

The Grammy category restructuring brings the question of what constitutes intertribal Native American music into the present moment and offers no easy answers. The distinction between historical and contemporary Native American musical genres is dependent upon individual, local, national, and international notions of musical Indianness. Attempting to generalize those into one single definition is as potentially problematic as trying to provide a singular definition for any other musical genre. That being said, Native American music is a foundational part of American musical culture and should be recognized as such. How can this best be accomplished in the context of an award like the Grammys?

I believe that you as reader, listener, producer, and consumer of music have a role to play in this discussion. The music you buy, the performances you attend, and the other ways in which you individually and communally circulate music have an effect on who is heard and who is not in our globalized music culture. The Native American musicians discussed here illustrate the many ways through which the genres of pow-wow, Native American flute, Native American pop and jazz have been made audible over time. I have characterized that audibility in relation to the work accomplished by the performers and their performances: sounding communities, sounding revitalization, sounding activism, and sounding unepxectedness.

The Grammy category restructuring points to future interactions and questions that are extremely relevant to intertribal Native American music. What does it mean to make Native American music? Is Native

American music a stylistic or ethnic-racial categorization and what positive and/or negative implications do those distinctions hold? Who listens to Native American music? What influence do performers have on audiences and audiences on performers? The Grammy category restructuring signals a moment, beyond the scope of the Recording Academy and the award, in which performers, listeners, and others associated with Native American music must discuss our experiences in order to understand how culture and musical performance have changed over time and the implications of those changes for the future audibility of Native American music. The purpose of this text has been to enter into that discussion with the idea of asking questions rather than giving answers. In that light, I end here with a question: How, after reading this book, do you define intertribal Native American music in the United States? For myself, I hope you will find value not in looking for *the* answer but instead in asking that question of yourself and others again and again in order to solicit new experiences and knowledge through which to grow in your life and in relation to others.

Glossary

Aboriginal Generalized term for Indigenous individuals and/or nations living in Canada.

Alaska Native Generalized term used to refer to Indigenous individuals and/or tribes living in Alaska, as distinct from American Indian.

American Indian Generalized term used to refer Indigenous individuals and/or tribes living in the contiguous United States.

Arena director Pow-wow staff member responsible for overseeing dancing and other events taking place within the dance arena.

Battle of Little Bighorn Battle between US 7th Cavalry and a combined force of Lakota, Cheyenne, and Arapaho, on June 25, 1876, fought over incursions into the Black Hills. The battle led to the the death of Lieutenant Colonel George A. Custer.

Beat In rhythm: equal-length durations or long or short subgroup in some systems of rhythmic grouping.

Block or **Bird** Carved piece of wood tied over anterior air chamber of Native American flute facilitating tone production.

Cadence Musical term for an ending.

Chord In tonal music, three or more pitches sounding together in a functional way; two or more intervals sounding together.

Chorus In musical structure, a long refrain added to a song verse; the main section of a popular song.

Circular time Concept of time in which past, present, and future are viewed as simultaneous instead of linear.

Culture (musical) Ways in which people make music meaningful and useful in their lives.

Drum One of various types of membranophones. Drum may also refer to the singing group with a specific pow-wow drum.

Ensemble Musical group.

First Nations One of three Indigenous groups recognized by the Canadian Constitution of 1982, the other two being Inuit and Métis.

Flag song Type of pow-wow song used to honor and recognize the flags carried in at the beginning of the pow-wow Grand Entry processional.

Frequency (pitch) In acoustics, the rate of vibration (cycles per second) in a string, column of air, or other sound-producing body.

Genre A type of music.

Giveaways Part of a general emphasis among Native American people on gift giving, a "giveaway" may refer to a pow-wow event at which gifts are given to those who contribute to the event, sometimes including virtually all attendees.

Gourd dance Southern Plains veteran's society dance that, in some areas, has been incorporated into the opening sequence of events at a pow-wow as a means of acknowledging military service and preparing the dance arena for a pow-wow.

Grand entry Opening processional at a pow-wow, during which all assembled dancers dance into the arena together. Some tribal cultures see grand entry as having been borrowed from Wild West shows. Grand entry line-up order is determined by local protocol as mediated by the Arena director.

Head dancers Female and male dancers who are invited by pow-wow committee members to lead the dancing at a given pow-wow and, in doing so, to act as public representatives of that pow-wow in publicity and on the day of the event. Depending upon pow-wow size, head dancers may also be selected across different age groups (head man, head woman, head golden age, etc.)

Honor beats Accented beats performed by one drummer in the course of a pow-wow song. Usually inserted during the B section, but they can be placed according to the tribal or intertribal practices of the drum in question. Honor beats are sometimes described as moment in which dancers "honor" the drum.

Honor song Type of pow-wow song used to honor particular individuals or moments in intertribal American Indian history.

Host drums Similar to head dancers, host drums are drum groups that are invited to lead the singing at a pow-wow and, in doing so, to publicly represent that pow-wow in publicity and on the day of the event. Depending on pow-wow size a committee might invite one or multiple host drums.

Improvisation Result of a musician exercising great flexibility with given material.

Indian Wars Conflicts between American Indian tribes, settlers, and the US federal government, sometimes portrayed in popular culture as concluding with the Wounded Knee massacre.

Indigeneity Quality or state of being Indigenous.

Indigenous From or native to a certain place.

Instrumentation Grouping of instruments used in a musical selection.

Intertribal As opposed to pan-Indian, a term derived from pow-wow practice to describe the various processes of cultural exchange that inform pow-wow practices.

Intertribal song Type of pow-wow song used for social dancing where all dance styles participate together, differentiated from round dance by its straight beat and forward facing heel-toe step.

Key In tonal music, a tonality named after the main pitch.

Master of ceremonies Also referred to as the MC or emcee, an individual who is invited by a pow-wow committee to narrate, explain, and to some degree mediate the similarities and differences between the various tribal and intertribal events taking place at a pow-wow to dancers and spectators.

Melody Any selection of pitches in succession. A "melody" is a particular succession of pitches.

Misogyny Hatred of women.

Musician A person who experiences music as practice.

Musicking From musicologist Christopher Small, "to take part, in any capacity, in a musical performance, whether by performing, by listening, by rehearsing or practicing, by providing material for performance (what is called composing), or by dancing" (Small 1998, 9).

Native American Generalized term used to refer to Indigenous individuals and/or tribes living in the United States.

Northern Plains Geographic distinction used in pow-wow singing practice to indicate a higher-pitched style of singing, as opposed to Southern Plains. Can also be used in reference to tribal or intertribal pow-wow practices emerging from states on the Northern Plains of the United States up into Canada.

Pan-Indian As opposed to intertribal, an anthropologically derived term that can be used to describe the various processes of cultural exchange that inform pow-wow practices as well as other aspects of American Indian history over time.

Pentatonic Systematic set of five pitches.

Peyote A hallucinogenic cactus whose sacred consumption is protected under the American Indian Religious Freedom Act.

Phrase Usually, melodic unit; a musical thought.

Pitch The quality of "highness" or "lowness" of sound; a sound produced at a certain number of cycles per second.

Polyphony "Multiple voices"; musical texture of two or more melodic parts performed together

Pow-wow An intertribal Native American event based upon a shared repertoire of songs and dances emerging from tribal ceremonial societies with secular and sacred implications for participants.

Pow-wow committee The pow-wow committee is the body responsible for facilitating pow-wow planning by selecting a theme, venue, head staff, vendors, and security.

Pulse Repeated articulations of equal durations.

Push-up One iteration of a pow-wow song melody.

Refrain Repeating text and melody added to a verse.

Relocation While Native relocation has taken place at many historical moments in time, the term in this case is often used as a shorthand way to refer to the Federal Relocation Program of the 1950s and 1960s that offered financial incentives for Indian people to relocate from their reservation homes to urban centers.

Rhythm Any succession of durations. A "rhythm" is a particular succession of durations.

Round dance song Type of pow-wow song used for social dancing, characterized by its heavily accented beat: 1 **2** 1 **2** 1 **2**.

Ruffle beat Rapid tremolo drum beat performed at loud and quiet dynamic levels, used in sneak-up songs as well as at the conclusion of flag songs.

Scale Pitch set (and therefore arrangement of intervals) presented in straight ascending or descending order.

Sneak-up song Type of pow-wow song that can be used in multiple dance contexts to reenact and honor experiences in battle or for general contest/exhibition dancing, characterized by a repeating pattern of **ruffle beat** followed by straight beat dancing.

Solo Performance by one person; a musical part meant to stand out.

Soundings Inspired by musicologist Christopher Small, soundings is a theoretical lens through which to look and listen to recordings not as objects but as the product of social relationships between groups of people.

Southern Plains Geographic distinction used in pow-wow singing practice to indicate a lower-pitched style of singing, as opposed to Northern Plains. Can also be used in reference to tribal or inter-tribal pow-wow practices emerging from states on the Southern Plains of the United States.

Speed The rate of the basic beats.

Staff notation Western system of notating music on a five-line staff.

Straight Beat pow-wow song dance beat characterized by a "straight" or regular pulse: 1 2 1 2 1 2. The second beat is still accented but not as heavily as in the round dance beat.

Structure Shape of a musical selection; form.

Style The combination of qualities that create distinctiveness.

Texture Musical relationships among ensemble parts.

Timbre Particular quality of sound; tone color.

Tone *See* Pitch.

Tuning Pitches to which an instrument is set.

Vibrato Pitch undulation controlled by singer or performer for expressive effect.

Victory song Type of pow-wow song used to honor and reenact deeds of bravery in battle.

Vocable Syllables used to convey a vocal melody, also defined by Wade as "song text syllables that are not linguistically meaning-ful" (Wade 2009, 215)

Wounded Knee massacre Massacre of the Lakota by the US 7th Cavalry on December 29, 1890.

Wounded Knee II Occupation of the town of the town of Wounded Knee, South Dakota, by the American Indian Movement, in 1973.

References

Ake, David Andrew. 2002. *Jazz Cultures*. Berkeley: University of California Press.

Battiste, Marie, and James [Sa'ke'j] Youngblood Henderson. 2000. *Protecting Indigenous Knowledge and Heritage: A Global Challenge, Purich's Aboriginal Issues Series*. Saskatoon, Saskatchewan: Purich Publishing.

Brockman, Joshua. 2002. *Arts in America; Beyond Drumbeats: New Sounds from Indian Country*. *New York Times*, January 16, 2002. http://www.nytimes.com/2002/01/16/arts/arts-in-america-beyond-drumbeats-new-sounds-from-indian-country.html?src=pm.

Browner, Tara. 2002. *Heartbeat of the People: Music and Dance of the Northern Pow-wow*. Urbana: University of Illinois Press.

———. 2009. *Music of First Nations: Tradition and Innovation in Native North America*. Urbana: University of Illinois Press.

Cajete, Gregory. 2000. *Native Science: Natural Laws of Interdependence*. Santa Fe: Clear Light.

Conlon, Paula. 1983. "The flute of the Canadian Amerindian: An analysis of the vertical whistle flute with external block and its music." Unpublished MA thesis, Carleton University, Ottawa, Canada.

———. 2002. "The Native American flute: Convergence and collaboration as exemplified by R. Carlos Nakai." *World of Music* 44 (1): 61–74.

———. 2009. "Nevaquaya, Joyce Lee 'Doc' Tate (1932–1996)." *Encyclopedia of Oklahoma History and Culture*. http://digital.library.okstate.edu/encyclopedia/entries/N/NE004.html, accessed August 11, 2012.

Deloria, Philip. 2004. *Indians in Unexpected Places*. Lawrence: University Press of Kansas.

Deloria, Jr., Vine. 1969. *Custer Died for Your Sins: An Indian Manifesto*. Norman: University of Oklahoma Press. Reprint, 1988.

Diamond, Beverley. 2002. "Native American contemporary music: The women." *World of Music* 44 (1): 11–39.

———. 2005. "Media as social action: Native American musicians in the recording studio." In *Wired for Sound: Engineering and Technologies in Sonic Cultures*, edited by Paul D. Greene and Thomas Porcello, 118–37. Middletown: Wesleyan University Press.

———. 2007. "The music of modern indigeneity: From identity to alliance studies." *European Meetings in Ethnomusicology* 12 (22): 169–90.

———. 2008. *Native American Music in Eastern North America*. Global Music Series, edited by Bonnie Wade and Patricia Shehan Campbell. New York: Oxford University Press.

Diamond, Beverley, M. Sam Cronk, and Franziska von Rosen. 1994. "Relationship, complementarity, and 'twinness.'" In *Visions of Sound: Musical Instruments of First Nations Communities in Northeastern America*. Chicago: University of Chicago Press.

Durham, Jimmie. 1993. "A certain lack of coherence." In *A Certain Lack of Coherence*, edited by Jean Fisher. London: Kala Press.

Ellis, Clyde. 1990. "'Truly dancing their own way': Modern revival and diffusion of the gourd dance." *American Indian Quarterly* 14 (1): 19–33.

———. 2003. *A Dancing People: Powwow Culture on the Southern Plains*. Lawrence: University Press of Kansas.

Ellis, Clyde, and Luke Eric Lassiter. 2005. Introduction. In *Powwow*, edited by Clyde Ellis, Luke Eric Lassiter, and Gary H. Dunham. Lincoln: University of Nebraska Press.

Ellis, Clyde, Luke Eric Lassiter, and Gary H. Dunham. 2005. *Powwow*. Lincoln: University of Nebraska Press.

Everything Is Everything. 1969. *Everything Is Everything, featuring Chris Hills*. Vanguard Apostolic VSD-6512. LP.

Fixico, Donald Lee. 1986. *Termination and Relocation: Federal Indian Policy, 1945–1960*. Albuquerque: University of New Mexico Press.

———. 2000. *The Urban Indian Experience in America*. Albuquerque: University of New Mexico Press.

Forbes, Jack D. 2001. "The urban tradition among Natives." In *American Indians and the Urban Experience*, edited by Susan Lobo and Kurt Peters. Walnut Creek: Altamira.

Gelo, Daniel J. 2005. "Powwow patter: Indian emcee discourse on power and identity." In *Powwow*, edited by Clyde Ellis, Luke Eric Lassiter, and Gary H. Dunham, 130–51. Lincoln: University of Nebraska Press.

Goldmark, Daniel. 2005. *Tunes for 'Toons: Music and the Hollywood Cartoon*. Berkeley: University of California Press.

Hardorff, Richard G. 2004. *Indian Views of the Custer Fight: A Source Book*. Norman: University of Oklahoma Press.

Harjo, Joy. 2002. *How We became Human: New and Selected Poems: 1975–2001*. New York: Norton.

Hercules, Bob, and Bob Jackson. 1999. *Songkeepers*. America's Flute Productions VHS.

Hoefnagels, Anna. 2012. "Aboriginal women and the Powwow drum." In *Aboriginal Music in Contemporary Canada: Echoes and Exchanges*, edited by Anna Hoefnagels and Beverley Diamond. Ithaca: McGill-Queen's University Press.

Howard, James H. 1955. "Pan-Indian culture of Oklahoma." *Scientific Monthly* 81 (5): 215–20.

Isaacs, Tony. 2005. "American Indian or Native American? I'm confused." http://indianhouse.com/essay_detail.php?title=American Indian or Native American? I'm Confused, accessed December 22, 2012

Johnson, Janis. 2010. "Performing Indianness and excellence: Nez Perce jazz bands of the twentieth century." In *American Indian Performing Arts: Critical Directions*, edited by Hanay Geiogamah and Jaye T. Darby, 197–222. Los Angeles: UCLA American Indian Studies Center.

———. 2008. *The Occupation of Alcatraz Island: Indian Self-determination and the Rise of Indian Activism*. 2nd ed. Urbana: University of Illinois Press. [Original edition, 1996].

Johnson, Troy, Duane Champagne, and Joane Nagel. 1997. "American Indian activism and transformation: Lessons from Alcatraz." In *American Indian Activism: Alcatraz to the Longest Walk*, edited by Troy Johnson, Joane Nagel, and Duane Champagne, 9–44. Chicago: University of Illinois Press.

Kidwell, Clara Sue, and Alan Velie. 2005. *Native American Studies*. Introducing Ethnic Studies, edited by Robert Con Davis-Undiano. Lincoln: University of Nebraska.

King, Thomas. 2005. *The Truth about Stories: A Native Narrative*. Indigenous Americas, edited by Robert Warrior and Jace Weaver. Minneapolis: University of Minnesota Press.

La Farge, Oliver. 1930. *Laughing Boy*. Boston: Houghton Mifflin.

Lassiter, Luke E. 1998. *The Power of Kiowa Song: A Collaborative Ethnography*. Tucson: University of Arizona Press.

Leventhal, Alan, Hank Alvarez, Monica Arellano, Carolyn M. Sullivan, Concha Rodriquez, and Rosemary Cambra. 2012. "The Muwekma Ohlone tribe of the San Francisco Bay and Alcatraz and Angel Islands." http://www.coloredreflections.com/decades/Decade.cfm?Dec= 2&Typ=3&Sty=1&PID=1027, accessed August 13, 2012.

Levine, Victoria Lindsay. 1993. "Musical revitalization among the Choctaw." *American Music* 11 (4): 391–411.

Lobo, Susan, Sharon Mitchell Bennett, Charlene Betsillie, Joyce Keoke, Geraldine Martinez Lira, and Marilyn LaPlante St. Germaine. 2002. *Urban Voices: The Bay Area American Indian Community; Community History Project, Intertribal Friendship House, Oakland, California*. Sun Tracks: An American Indian Literary Series, vol. 50, edited by Ofelia Zepeda. Tucson: University of Arizona Press.

Lobo, Susan, and Kurt Peters. 2001. *American Indians and the Urban Experience*. Walnut Creek: Altimira.

Locke, Kevin. 1982. *Love Songs of the Lakota Performed on Flute by Kevin Locke*. Indian House CD IH 4315.

———. 2011. Personal communication.

Maas, Michele. 2012. Interview with John-Carlos Perea. San Francisco, California.

Madril, Eddie. 2012. Interview with John-Carlos Perea. San Francisco, California.

Madril, Marcos. 2012. Interview with John-Carlos Perea. San Francisco, California.

Mauchahty-Ware, Tom. 1978. *Flute Songs of the Kiowa and Comanche*. Indian House CD IH 2512.

McAllester, David P. 1949. *Peyote Music*. Viking Fund Publications in Anthropology, vol. 13, edited by Ralph Linton. New York: Viking Fund.

———. 1981. "New perspectives in Native American music." *Perspectives of New Music* 20 (1/2): 433–46.

———. 2005. Personal letter, October 25, 2005.

Moisa, Ray. 2002. "Relocation: The promise and the lie." In *Urban Voices: The Bay Area American Indian Community; Community History Project, Intertribal Friendship House, Oakland, California*, edited by Susan Lobo, Sharon Mitchell Bennett, Charlene Betsillie, Joyce Keoke, Geraldine Martinez Lira and Marilyn LaPlante St. Germaine, 21–8. Tucson: University of Arizona Press.

Nakai, R. Carlos. 1987. *Earth Spirit*. Canyon Records CD CR-612.

———. 1989. *Canyon Trilogy*. Canyon Records CD CR-610.

Nakai, R. Carlos, and James DeMars. 1997. *Two World Concerto*. Canyon Records CD CR-7016.

Nakai, R. Carlos, James DeMars, David McAllester, and Ken Light. 1996. *The Art of the Native American Flute*. Phoenix: Canyon Records Productions.

Nakai, R. Carlos. 2004. *Introduction*. Liner notes for *Comanche Flute Music Played by Doc Tate Nevaquaya*. Smithsonian Folkways Recordings SFW CD 50403: 1–2.

Nevaquaya, Doc Tate. 2004. *Comanche Flute Music Played by Doc Tate Nevaquaya*. Smithsonian Folkways Recordings SFW CD 50403.

Osawa, Sandra. 1997. *Pepper's Pow Wow*. USA: Upstream Productions. VHS.

Payne, Richard W. 1999. *The Native American Plains Flute*. Oklahoma City: Toubat Trails.

Perea, Jessica Bissett. 2011. "The Politics of Inuit Musical modernities in Alaska." Unpublished PhD diss., University of California, Los Angeles.

Perea, John-Carlos. 2009. *Witchi Tai To: An Historical Acoustemology*. Unpublished PhD diss., University of California, Berkeley.

———. 2012. "The Unexpectedness of Jim Pepper." *MUSICultures* no. 39 (1, Special Issue: Indigenous Modernities):70–82.

Pond, Steven F. 2005. *Head Hunters: The Making of Jazz's First Platinum Album*. Ann Arbor: University of Michigan Press.

Powers, William K. 1990. *War Dance: Plains Indian Musical Performance*. Tucson: University of Arizona Press.

Prucha, Francis Paul. 1986. *The Great Father: The United States Government and the American Indians*. Abridged ed. Lincoln: University of Nebraska Press.

Sainte-Marie, Buffy. 1964. *It's My Way*. Vanguard VSD-79142.

———. 2009. *Running for the Drum*. Appleseed Recordings APR CD 1117.

Scales, Christopher. 2007. "Powwows, intertribalism, and the value of competition." *Ethnomusicology* 51 (1): 1–29.

Schulman, Sandra Hale. 2011. "Goodbye Native Grammy: NARAS dumps hard earned category." *News from Indian Country*. http://indiancountry news.net/cultures/283-reviews/11754-goodbye-native-grammy-naras-dumps-hard-earned-category., accessed August 16, 2012.

Shreve, Bradley G. 2011. *Red Power Rising: The National Indian Youth Council and the Origins of Native Activism*. Norman: University of Oklahoma Press.

Sissons, Jeffrey. 2005. *First Peoples: Indigenous Cultures and their Futures*. London: Reaktion.

Small, Christopher. 1998. "Prelude: Music and musicking." In *Musicking: The Meanings of Performing and Listening*. Hanover, NH: Wesleyan University Press.

Smith, Lawrence R. 1988. "An interview with Jim Pepper." *Caliban* 5: 150–71.

Smith, Paul Chaat. 2009. *Everything You Know about Indians is Wrong*. Minneapolis: University of Minnesota Press.

Smith, Paul Chaat, and Robert Allen Warrior. 1996. *Like a Hurricane: The Indian Movement from Alcatraz to Wounded Knee*. New York: New Press.

Strauss, Neil. 2001. "The pop life; Native genre takes pride of place at the Grammys." *New York Times*, February 21. http://www.nytimes.com/2001/02/21/arts/the-pop-life-native-genre-takes-pride-of-place-at-the-grammys.html?src=pm.

Tangen, Rulan. 2012. Interview with John-Carlos Perea. San Francisco, California.

Taruskin, Richard. 2009. "Yevreyi and Zhidy: A memoir, a survey, and a plea." In *On Russian Music*. Berkeley: University of California Press.

Titon, Jeff Todd, and Mark Slobin. 1996. "The music-culture as a world of music." In *Worlds of Music: An Introduction of the Music of the World's Peoples*, edited by Jeff Todd Titon, 1–16. New York: Schirmer.

Troutman, John W. 2009. *Indian Blues: American Indians and the Politics of Music, 1879–1934*. Norman: University of Oklahoma Press.

Vennum, Thomas., Jr. 1982. *The Ojibwa Dance Drum*, Smithsonian Folklife Studies. Washington, DC: Smithsonian Institution Press.

Vizenor, Gerald. 2008. "Aesthetics of survivance: Literary theory and practice." In *Survivance: Narratives of Native Presence*, edited by Gerald Vizenor. Lincoln: University of Nebraska Press.

Wade, Bonnie C. 2009. *Thinking Musically: Expressing Music, Experiencing Culture*. 2nd ed. Global Music Series. New York: Oxford University Press.

Wapp, Edward, Jr. 1984. "The American Indian Courting Flute: Revitalization and Change." In *Sharing a Heritage*, edited by Charlotte Heth and Michael Swarm. Los Angeles: UCLA American Indian Studies Center.

Wapp, Edward R. 1984. "The Sioux courting flute: Its tradition, construction, and music." Unpublished MA thesis Music, University of Washington.

White, Glenn H., Bill Koomsa Sr., and Ernest Toppah. 1998. *Traditional Kiowa Songs. Liner Notes for Kiowa: Traditional Kiowa Songs*. Canyon Records CR-6145.

Wright-McLeod, Brian. 2005. *The Encyclopedia of Native Music*. Tucson: University of Arizona Press.

XIT. 1972. *Plight of the Redman*. Rare Earth R-536. LP.

Young Bear, Severt, and R. D. Theisz. 1994. *Standing in the Light: A Lakota Way of Seeing*. Lincoln: University of Nebraska Press.

Young, Gloria. 1981. "Powwow Power: Perspectives on historic and contemporary intertribalism." Unpublished PhD diss., Indiana University.

Youngblood, Mary. 2002. *Beneath the Raven Moon*: Silver Wave Records CD SD 931. Liner notes for Beneath the Raven Moon, Silver Wave Records CD SD 931.

Resources

Record Labels

http://www.canyonrecords.com. Canyon Records is one of the oldest producers and distributors of Native American music based in Phoenix, Arizona.

http://www.silverwave.com/index.shtml. Silverwave is an independent music label for Native American, World, and New Age music.

http://www.indianhouse.com. Indian House Records specializes in traditional Native American and pow-wow musics.

http://www.folkways.si.edu. The nonprofit record label of the Smithsonian Institution.

Musicians and Dancers

http://www.facebook.com/pages/Elk-Soldier/45003108858?v=info. Elk Soldier drum group.

http://www.facebook.com/pages/Porcupine-Singers/337905748679? v=info. Porcupine Singers drum group.

http://www.myspace.com/therealblacklodgesingers. Blacklodge Singers drum group.

http://www.myspace.com/youngbird97. Youngbird drum group.

http://www.northerncree.com. Northern Cree Singers are a First Nations powwow drum based from the Saddle Lake Cree Nation.

http://www.kevinlocke.com/kevin/index.html. Personal website for Lakota and Anishinabe flutist Kevin Locke.

http://www.rcarlosnakai.com. Personal website for Navajo and Ute flutist R. Carlos Nakai.

http://www.maryyoungblood.com. Personal website for Seminole and Aleut flutist Mary Youngblood.

http://www.creative-native.com. Personal website for Cree artist and musician Buffy Sainte-Marie.

http://www.floydredcrowwesterman.com. Personal website for Dakota musician and artist Floyd Red Crow Westerman.

http://jimpepperlives.wordpress.com. Online resource for information about the life and music of Creek and Kaw musician Jim Pepper.

http://www.blackfire.net. Website for Navajo punk trio Blackfire.

http://www.atribecalledred.com. Website for electronic dance music DJs A Tribe Called Red.

http://www.hoopman4.com. Website for pow-wow dancer and educator Eddie Madril featured in chapter 2.

http://www.dancingearth.org. Website for Dancing Earth Dance company led by dancer and choreographer Rulan Tangen featured in chapter 2.

http://www.xitoriginal.com. Website for the Original XIT Boyz featuring the surviving members of XIT featured in chapter 4.

http://www.powwows.com. Online community for Native American tribes, history, pow wows, culture, music and art.

http://www.nativeamericanmusicawards.com/home.cfm. Home of the NAMMYs.

http://www.grammy.com. Official site of the National Academy of Recording Arts and Sciences, which hosts the Grammy Awards.

http://www.indiansummer.org. Summer music festival in Milwaukee, Wisconsin.

General

http://www.paulchaatsmith.com. Personal website for Comanche author, essayist, and curator Paul Chaat Smith.

http://nmai.si.edu/home. National Museum of the American Indian.

http://www.isuma.tv. A free video site and internet portal devoted to Indigenous filmmakers.

http://ericalord.com/home.html. Personal website for Athabascan, Iñupiaq, Finnish, Swedish, English, and Japanese artist Erica lord.

http://naisa.org/. Homepage for the Native American and Indigenous Studies Association.

http://www.ankn.uaf.edu. A resource for compiling and exchanging information related to Alaska Native knowledge systems and ways of knowing.

http://www.nativefederation.org. Site for Alaska Federation of Natives, the largest statewide organization whose membership includes 178 villages, thirteen regional corporations, and twelve regional nonprofit and tribal consortiums.

http://www.friendshiphousesf.org. Online site for the Association of American Indians Inc. of San Francisco.

http://www.ifhurbanrez.org. Online resource for the Intertribal Friendship House located in Oakland, California.

http://www.nativehealth.org. The Native American Health Center is a nonprofit organization serving the California Bay Area Native Population and other underserved populations in the Bay Area.

http://www.baaits.org. Website for Bay Area American Indian Two-Spirits.

http://www.trc.ca/websites/trcinstitution/index.php?p=3. The Truth and Reconciliation Commission of Canada has a mandate to learn the truth about what happened in the residential schools and to inform all Canadians about what happened in the schools.

http://www.idlenomore.ca. Website for Idle No More movement in Canada.

http://www.worldflutes.org. Website for the International Native American Flute Association.

VHS/DVD

Musicians

Banner, Chuck, and Floyd Red Crow Westerman. 2001. *XIT without reservation*. Albuquerque, NM: Warrior.

Littlejohn, Hawk, Kevin Locke, R. Carlos Nakai, Tom Mauchahty-Ware, Sonny Nevaguaya, and Richard Payne. 1999. *Songkeepers: A Saga of Five Native Americans, Told Through the Sound of the Flute*. Lake Forest, IL: America's Flute Productions.

Osawa, Sandy Sunrising. 1995. *Pepper's Pow Wow*. Seattle, WA: Upstream Productions.

Sainte-Marie, Buffy, Gilles Paquin, Joan Prowse, John Bessai, and John Einarson. 2006. *Buffy Sainte-Marie: A Multimedia Life*. Toronto: CineFocus.

Schulman, Sandra Hale, Delores Smith, Kevin Welch, Peter La Farge, June Carter Cash, Johnny Cash, Pete Seeger, and Karen Dalton. 2010. *The Ballad of Peter La Farge*. Nashville: Slink Productions.

Swearington, Scott. 1992. *Into the Circle*. Tulsa: Full Circle Communications.

Torrie, Jeremy, and Jules Desjarlais. 2004. *Pow wow Trail*. Winnipeg, Manitoba: Arbor Records.

Williams, Marla, Martin Sheen, and Mary Youngblood. 2005. *Aleut Story*. Lincoln, NE: Aleutian-Pribilof Heritage.

General

Diamond, Neil, Catherine Bainbridge, Jeremiah Hayes, Christina Fon, Linda Ludwick, Clint Eastwood, Jim Jarmusch, et al. 2010. *Reel Injun*. Canada: Distributed in Canada by Mongrel Media.

Duncan, Dalina, and Pratap Chatterjee. 2003. *Gold, greed & genocide the untold tragedy of the California Gold Rush*. Berkeley, CA: Oyate.

Eyre, Chris, Larry Estes, Scott Rosenfelt, B. C. Smith, Adam Beach, Evan Adams, Irene Bedard et al. 2000. *Smoke Signals*. United States: Miramax Home Entertainment.

Grimberg, Sharon, Cathleen O'Connell, Anne Makepeace, Mark Zwonitzer, Chris Eyre, Ric Burns, Rob Rapley, et al. 2009. *We Shall Remain: America Through Native Eyes*. Boston: WGBH Educational Foundation.

Index

∞

AIM song, 23
Ake, David, 92
Akimel O'odham, 91, 99
Akwesasne Notes, 77
Alaska Federation of Natives, 12
"Alcatraz" (Redbone), 86, 87
Alaska Native, 11, 12
Alcatraz Island
   occupation of, 10, 23, 75, 78–79, 82, 88–89
   original name of, 74
   Sunrise Ceremony at, 74, 75
Aleut, 57, 71
   forced relocation from the Aleutian
      Chain, 72
Aleut Story (Youngblood), 72
All-Star Band, 99
   See also Armstrong
American Indian
   as a term, 10–11, 12
   Civil Rights movement of, 23
      See also political activism; Red Power
         movement
American Indian Federation (AIF), 77, 78
American Indian Movement (AIM), 23, 78,
      84, 88
Anishinabe, 66
Apache, 10, 49, 77
   Jicarilla, 12
   Mescalero, 11, 14, 24, 59
   White Mountain, 6
Arapaho, 1
Arizona Musical Instrument Museum
   "I am AZ Music," 100
Armstrong, Louis, 95, 99
   All-Star Band, 99
   and Dixieland, 100
   "Basin Street Blues," 100
   "Bell Telephone Hour, The," 99
   High Button Shoes, 100
      "I Still Get Jealous," 100
   Louis Armstrong's Big Band and Sextet, 99

assimilation
   forced, 20
Atlanta Braves
   "Tomahawk Chop," 1
Attawapiskat, 90
Ayala, Manuel de, 74

Bailey, Mildred Eleanor [Rinker], 91, 98–99
   "Rockin' Chair," 98
bands, Native American, 97
Banks, Dennis, 78
"Basin Street Blues" (Armstrong), 100
Battle of Little Bighorn, 43, 80
   See also Custer, La Farge
bebop. *See* music
Bechet, Sidney, 99
Bee, Tom, 88
   Sound of America (SOAR) record label, 107
"Bell Telephone Hour, The." *See* Armstrong
Bellamy, Tony. *See* Redbone
Bellecourt, Clyde, 78
Beneath the Raven Moon. See Youngblood
Berenstain Bears, The. See Locke
Bering, Vitus, 12
Betty Boop cartoon
   Rhythm on the Reservation, 92
Billboard, 104
Bitsui, Sherwin, 1
Black Lodge Singers, 37
Blackfeet, 37
Blackfire, 3, 90
   One Nation Under, 90
Bless the People: Harmonized Peyote
      Songs, 107
Blue Horse Singers, 56
Boarding School Healing Project, 105
Bonin, Gertrude, 77
bop. *See* music
Browner, Tara, 19, 20, 21, 24, 25
   grand entry into pow wow, 32
   pow-wow dance styles, 29, 44

Buffalo Bill's Wild West, 21
Builds-The-Fire, Thomas, 1

Cajete, Gregory, 18
Calloway, Cab, 95
Canadian Constitution, 11
Canyon Records, 70
 See also Nakai
Canyon Trilogy. See Nakai
Capone, Al, 74
Carlisle Indian Industrial School, 96
Carmichael, Hoagy
 "Rockin' Chair," 98
cedar flute. *See* instruments
ceremonial societies, 20
Champagne, Duane, 77
Charette, Phillip, 73
Cherokee, 8, 91, 101
Cherry, Don, 104
Cheyenne, 1, 86
Chippewa, 44
Choctaw, 19, 91, 101
classical music. *See* music
Coeur d' Alene, 91, 98
Collier, John, Sr., 21
Columbus, Christopher, 12
Columbus Day. *See* Indigenous Peoples Day
Comanche, 57, 63, 64, 65, 78, 104
Comanche Flute Music, (Nevaquaya), 64
"Come and Get Your Love" (Redbone), 86
"Coming of the Whiteman, The" (XIT), 88
Conlon, Paula, 57, 58, 60
Cook, James, 12
Coom, Chris Ti, 72
 See also Youngblood
Cornplanter, 83
Cornwall International Bridge blockade, 77
Coryell, Larry, 103
 See also Pepper
country music. *See* music
"Courting Song," (Mauchahty-Ware), 66
Cozad, Belo, 65
Crazy Horse, 81
 See also Battle of Little Bighorn, Custer
Cree, 76, 93
 Hobbema, 3
 Northern, 11, 12
Creek, 1, 91, 102
Cronk, Sam
 significance of women in a pow wow
  circle, 27
Crosby, Bing, 98
"Custer," (La Farge), 80–82

Custer Died for Your Sins (Deloria),
 84–86, 87
Custer, General George Armstrong, 43,
 80–81, 86

Dakota, 5, 32, 75, 77, 88, 107
dance
 bans on, 20
 California Indian dance, 28
 Gourd, 31–32
 danza Azteca, 28
 See also pow wow
Dance with the Wind. See Youngblood
DANCING EARTH Indigenous
  Contemporary Dance
  Creations, 48
 See also Tangen
Delaware, 13
Deloria, Philip J., 1, 5, 12, 91–92, 97
Deloria, Vine, 84
 Custer Died for Your Sins, 84
DeMars, James
 Two World Concerto, 70, 71
DePoe, Pete. *See* Redbone
Diamond, Beverley, 11, 12, 70
 alliance studies, 75, 76, 90
 Global Music Series, 12
 *Native American Music in Eastern North
  America,* 1
 on Mary Youngblood, 72
 significance of women in a pow wow
  circle, 27
Diamond, Neil, 93
 *Reel Injun: On the Trail of the Hollywood
  Indian,* 93
Dion, Shane
 "Facebook Drama," 42
Dion, Twila
 "Facebook Drama," 42
Dixieland. *See* music
drums
 construction of, 25–26
 See also instruments, pow wow
Dunham, Gary H., 20
Durham, Jimmie, 8
Dylan, Bob, 80, 82, 91

Earth Spirit. See Nakai
Eastman, Charles, 77
Elk
 "Hoka Hey," 32
Ellington, Duke, 102
 See also Pettiford

Ellis, Clyde, 9–10, 20, 21
  Gourd Dance, 31–32
  pow-wow dance styles, 29, 44
Employment Assistance Program, 79
"End?" (XIT), 88, 89
Epic Records, 86
Eskimo. *See* Inuit
Everything Is Everything, 103, 104
  See also Pepper
Eyre, Chris
  Smoke Signals, 1

"Facebook Drama," 39, 40, 41, 106
  lyrics to, 42
First Nations, 11, 12, 40
  round dances, 41
fish-ins. *See* Pacific Northwest Indian
      fishing rights
Fixico, Donald Lee, 9, 22, 78, 79
Fleischer cartoon studio, 93, 05
flute
  American Indian, 59
  and precursor whistles, 61
  as a social activity, 60
  block, 61, 72
  made for specific tribal music, 59
  made in specific keys, 58
    pentatonic scale of, 58
  Native American, 56–73
    construction of, 58 fig. 3.1
    description of, 57
    origin stories, 61–62
    elk in, 62
    revitalization of, 60–61
  See also instruments; Nevaquaya; pow wow
Flute Songs of the Kiwa and Commanche,
      (Mauchahty-Ware), 65
"Flute Wind Song" (Nevaquaya), 64, 65
folk music. *See* music
Follkways Records, 80
  See also La Farge
Forbes, Jack, 13, 79
Ford, John, 1
Four Circles, 24
Free Spirits, The, 103
Freeman, Cassandra, 92
Friendship House Association of American
      Indians, San Francisco, 23, 79
Fuentes, Tony, 51

Gall, Chief, 81
  See also Battle of Little Bighorn, Custer
Garris, R. C., 88

Gathering of Nations. *See* pow wow
Gelo, Daniel J., 53
genocide, 20
Geronimo (Nakai), 70
Getz, Stan, 102
  See also Pettiford
Gila River Indian Community, 99
Gila River Reservation, 100
  Russell Moore Music Festival, 100
Gillespie, Dizzy, 101
Global Music Series (Diamond), 12
Goldmark, Daniel, 95
  *Tunes for 'Toons: Music and the Hollywood
      Cartoon*, 93
Goodfeather, Jeremy, 75
Goodman, Benny, 98
Gourd, 31–32
Grammy awards, 107, 108
  Best Native American Album, 107
  Regional Roots category, 108
  See also Nakai; Youngblood
Gushoney, Florinda, 6
Gushoney, Orlando, 6

Hampton, Lionel, 99
Hardoff, Richard G., 81
Harjo, Joy, 1
Hercules, Bob, 65
Herrera, Leeja, 88
High Button Shoes, 100
  See also Armstrong, Moore
Hills, Chris, 103
  "Witchi Tai To," 103, 104
  See also Pepper
hip hop. *See* music
Hoefnagels, Anna, 27
Hoehner, Bernard, 14, 19, 20
  and community service, 42
  and four circles of a pow wow, 25
  and lyrics to "The Photograph," 68
  and male singer behavior, 27
  and pow-wow etiquette, 24
  and sneak-up songs, 39
  and the cedar flute, 56, 67
  as a WWII veteran, 21
  block flute, 61
  Blue Horse Singers, 28
  flag song translation by, 34, 35
    See also Sweetwater Singers
  image, 15 fig.1.3
  origin stories and, 62, 66
"Hoka Hey" (Elk Soldier), 32
"Home of the Warriors," 38

Honoring Singers, 41 fig. 2.5
Howard, James H., 9
Hunkpapa, 14

#IdleNoMore movement, 77, 90
Indian Flute Songs from Comanche Land,
   (Nevaquaya) 64
Indian House Records, 58, 65, 67
Indian Wars, 20
Indian
   as a term, 10–11
Indians in Unexpected Places (Deloria), 91
Indians of All Tribes, 23, 74, 80
   See also Alcatraz Island occupation
indigeneity, 13
Indigenous Peoples Day, 80
instruments
   cedar flute, 4, 5, 6, 14, 56–73
   description of, 57
   drums, 11, 14
   See also pow wow
International Indian Treaty Council, 84
intertribal, 9–10
   exchange, 11–12
Intertribal Friendship House, Oakland, CA,
   22, 79–80
Inuit, 11, 12
Ironwood Singers, 39
   image, 40 fig. 2.4
   "Little Bighorn Victory Song," 42
Iroquois, 75
Isaacs, Tony, 58, 59, 65, 66
It's My Way (Sainte-Marie), 82

Jackson, Bob, 65
Jackson Five, "We've Got Blue
   Skies," 88
jazz. *See* music
Johnson, Janis, 97
Johnson, Tim, 99
Johnson, Troy, 23, 74, 77, 78, 79
Joseph, Victor, 1

Kaw, 91, 102
Keefe, Julia, 99
Kevin Locke Native Dance Ensemble, 67
Kidwell, Clara Sue, 77
Kinzua Dam, 83
   See also Sainte-Marie
Kiowa, 24, 52, 57, 65
   Flag Song, 36
Koomsa, Bill, Sr., 36

La Farge, Oliver
   Laughing Boy, 80
La Farge, Peter, 76, 80–82, 84, 86, 87
   Greenwich Village folk scene, 80, 91
   wartime awards, 80
"Lake that Speaks." *See* Nakai
Lakota, 24, 36, 51, 57, 66
   dream societies and, 62
   language, 34
   National Anthem, 35
   Standing Rock, 59
Lakota Language Consortium, 67
land, importance of, 13–15
Lassiter, Luke, 9–10, 20, 44
   Gourd Dance, 31–32
Laughing Boy (La Farge), 80
Leventhal, Alan, 74
Levine, Victoria Lindsay, 56, 60
Lincoln Street Exit. *See* XIT
"Little Bighorn Victory Song,"
   lyrics, 42–43
Lobo, Susan, 9, 22
Locke, Kevin, 57, 58, 59
   as a flutist, 66–68, 70, 71
   recording *The Berenstain Bears*, 67
Louis Armstrong's Big Band and Sextet, 99
   See also Armstrong
Louis Bull Reserve, 41 fig. 2.5
Love Songs of the Lakota, 67

Maas, Michele
   women's Jingle Dress, 44
Madril, Eddie, 45–48, 46 fig. 2.6
Madril, Marcos, 50–52
Maidu, 74
Martin, A. Michael, 88, 89
Mashpee Wampanoag, 49
Mauchahty-Ware, Tom, 57, 65–66, 67, 70
McAllester, David P., 88
   See also XIT
Means, Russell, 78
Métis, 11
"Midnight at Bohemia" (Pettiford), 102
Mike, Johnny
   Bless the People: Harmonized Peyote Songs, 107
Mi'kmaq, 82
Miwok, 74
Mohawk, 77, 80, 99
Moisa, Ray, 79
Monk, Thelonious, 102
   See also Pettiford
Montezuma, Carlos, 77

Moore, Russell "Big Chief," 91, 99–100
  "Basin Street Blues," 100
  "Bell Telephone Hour, The," 99
  High Button Shoes, 100
  "I Still Get Jealous," 100
  See also Armstrong; Russell Moore Music
    Festival
Moses, Bob, 103
  See also Pepper
Motown Records, 88, 01
music
  American Indian, 59
    as entertainment for non-Natives, 21
  as a social activity, 14
  bebop, 102
  bop, 101
  cedar flute, 4, 5, 6, 56–73
  classical, 1, 14
  country, 3
  Dixieland, 100
  folk, 4
  hip hop, 3, 90
  Irish, 14
  jazz, 1, 3, 14, 91–105
  musica tejana, 14
  Native American
    flute, 1, 56–73
      description of, 57
      sound of, 1
    pow-wow, 14, 15, 16–55
      as a sounding, 1, 3, 4, 5, 6, 12
      intertribal, 9, 13
  punk rock, 3, 90
  recording industry, 21
  revitalization of, 60
  rock, 1
  staff notation, 30
  See also pow wow
Muwekma Ohlone, 74

Nagel, Joane, 77
Nakai, R. Carlos, 56, 57, 68–71, 71, 107, 108
  Canyon Trilogy, 70
  Earth Spirit, 70
  Geronimo, 70
  Grammy nominations, 70
  image, 69 fig. 3.3
  "Lake that Speaks," 70
  The New World, 70
  "Shaman's Call," 70
Narragansett, 76, 80
Navaho, 1, 56, 68, 90

National Congress of American Indians
    (NCAI), 77–78, 84
National Indian Youth Council (NIYC), 23, 78
National Museum of the American Indian, 99
  "Up Where We Belong," 100
Native American, 10–11
  *Native American Music in Eastern North
    America* (Diamond), 1
Native American Studies, 78
Navajo, 1, 3, 107
Navajo Beauty Way ceremony, 104
Nevaquaya, Joyce Lee "Doc" Tate, 57, 60, 63
    fig. 3.2
  as a floutist, 64, 65, 67, 69, 70, 71
  See also Comanche Flute Music
New World, The. See Nakai
Nez Perce, 99
Northern California Flute Circle, 72
  See also Youngblood
Northern Cree Singers, 38, 39, 41 fig. 2.5
  "Facebook Drama," 39, 40, 41, 106
Northern Yokut, 74
"Now that the Buffalo's Gone," (Sainte-
    Marie), 82, 84

Oakes, Richard, 80
occupations. *See* Alcatraz Island; Cornwall
    International Bridge; Wounded
    Knee II;
Odawa, 92
Office of Indian Affairs (OIA), 97
Oglala Lakota, 3, 21, 78
Ojibwe
  Leech Lake, 78
  White Earth, 78
One Nation Under (Blackfire), 90
origin stories. *See* flute; pow wow
Original XIT Boyz, The. *See* XIT
Ortiz, Simon, 1
Osage, 78

Pacific Northwest Indian fishing rights, 78
Paiute, 78
pan-Indian, 9–10
Pascua Yaqui, 45
"path, The," 104
Pawnee (OK), 37
Payne, Richard W., 57, 62, 65
Pepper, Jim, 91, 102–104, 105
  Everything Is Everything, 103
  Free Spirits, The, 103
  image, 103 fig. 5.2

Pepper, Jim (*continued*)
  "path, The," 104
  "Witchi Tai To," 103, 104
Perception Records, 85
Perea, John-Carlos, 9, 13, 68, 85 fig. 4.2,
    103, 104
Peters, Kurt, 22
Pettiford, Doc
  Doc Pettiford and his Family Orchestra, 101
  "Midnight at Bohemia," 102
  "Stardust," 102
Pettiford, Oscar, 91, 101–102
  image, 101 fig. 5.1
  New Oscar Pettiford Sextet, The, 101
Phillips, Tom, 52
"Photograph, The," (Locke) 67
  lyrics to, 68
  See also Love Songs of the Lakota
Pima, 91
Plight of the Redman (XIT), 88, 89
political activism, 76–80, 81–82
  See also Alcatraz Island occupation;
    Cornwall International Bridge;
    #IdleNoMore; Pacific Northwest
    Indian fishing rights; Red Power
    Movement; Trail of Broken Treaties;
    Wounded Knee II
Pomo, 74
Ponca, 78, 107
Porcupine Singers, 34, 35, 36
  "Veteran's Song (Victory Song for posting
    of the colors)," 37
Potlatch (Redbone), 86
Powhattan, 13
pow-wow, 13, 14
  arena director, 32, 52
  as a drug- and alcohol-free event, 53
  behavior of participants at, 26–27
  committee, 53
  contests, 38
  dancing in, 14, 17, 28, 43–52, 90
    ban on, 20
    bells on, 17
    contest, 38
    Gourd Dance, 31–32
    Men's Fancy Dance, 29, 45
    Men's Grass, 29, 45, 48
    Men's Southern Traditional, 29, 65
    Men's Northern traditional, 19, 51
    Pow Wow Step, 90
    round, 39
      Northern Plains, 39
    social, 37

Women's Buckskin, 28
Women's Cloth, 28
Women's Fancy Shawl, 28–29
Women's Jingle Dress, 28, 44
definition of, 18
drums in, 25, 90
  construction of, 25–26
  significance of materials, 26
  positioning at, 26 fig. 2.2
emcees in, 14, 19
flags in, 34
flyer, 54 fig. 2.7
food at, 16
four circles of, 25–26
Gathering of Nations, 24
grand entry into, 21, 32, 52
  shared by Northern and Southern Plains
    representatives, 36
head dancers, 53
host drums, 53
importance of, during WWII and the
    Vietnam War, 21–22
intertribal, 15
master of ceremonies, 53
misogyny in, 28
music, 16–55
Northern Plains, 19–20
singing, 17 fig. 2.1, 90
  female, 27
  honor beats, 33
  male, 26
    high voice significance, 27
  musical phrase, 34
  Northern Plains, 17, 19, 30–31, 42
    pitch and timbre of, 37
    reactions to, 31
    visual representation of song form, 32,
      33 fig. 2.3
  push-up
    as a melody, 32
    responsibilities of, 30
  Southern Plains, 17, 65
    pitch and timbre of, 37
    visual representation of song form, 32,
      33 fig. 2.3
  straight beat, 34
  vocables, 32, 33
songs
  contest, 38
  flag, 34, 35, 36
  "Home of the Warriors," 38
  honor, 42–43
  intertribal, 37

round dance, 39
  sneak-up, 38
  veteran's, 36, 37
  victory, 34, 35, 36, 37, 42
Southern Plains, 19–20
spectators at, 29–30
stories
  origin, 18–25, 61–62
    See also Red Power Movement
  elk in, 62
  See also flute
vendors at, 29, 53
  See also instruments, music
Powers, William K., 20, 33, 44
Pratt, Richard Henry, Lieutenant, 96
Primeau, Verdell
  *Bless the People: Harmonized Peyote
    Songs*, 107
  Grammy award, 107
Prucha, Francis Paul, 96
Public Enemy, 90
Pueblo, 88
  Acoma, 1
  Laguna, 88
  Taos, 88
punk rock. *See* music

Qur'an, 4

Rainer, John, Jr., 73
Ramone, Joey, 90
  One Nation Under, 90
  See also Blackfire
Rare Earth Records, 88
Red Bow, Buddy, 3
Red Cliff Band, 44
Red Power Movement, 23, 75, 86, 88, 89
  origin stories, 77–80
Redbone, 76, 86–87
  "Alcatraz," 86, 87
  "Come and Get Your Love," 86
  "Maggie," 87
  Potlatch, 86
Reel Injun: On the Trail of the Hollywood Indian
    (Diamond), 93
regalia, 49, 50
Relocation Program, Federal, 22
reservations, relocation to, 20
Resistance, The (War Party), 90
Rhodes, Willard, 67
Rhythm on the Reservation (Betty Boop), 92–96,
    98, 105
Rinker, Al, 98

"Road, The" (Tribe Called Red, A), 90
Robinson, Smokey, 88
Rock and Roll Hall of Fame. *See* Redbone
rock music. *See* music
"Rockin' Chair" (Bailey, Carmichael), 98
Romero, Robby, 88
Rosen, Franziska von, significance of women
    in a pow wow circle, 27
Running for the Drum (Sainte-Marie), 82
Russell Moore Music Festival, 100

Sac and Fox, 62
Sainte-Marie, Buffy, 12, 76, 82–84, 86,
    87, 90
  Greenwich Village folk music scene, 80,
    82, 91
  image, 83 fig. 4.1
  It's My Way, 82
  "Now that the Buffalo's Gone," 82
  Running for the Drum, 82
San Francisco Bay Area Urban Indian
    community, 44
Scales, Christopher, 38
Schulman, Sandra Hale, 108
Seeger, Pete, 80
Seminole, 57, 71
Seneca, 83
"Shaman's Call." (Nakai), 70
Shea Murphy, Jacqueline, 44
Sherman Institute, 99
Shoshone, 86
  Bannock, 80
Shreve, Bradley, 23, 77, 78
Sihása, 14
singing. *See* pow wow
  ruffle beat, 35, 38
Sioux, 92
Sioux Treaty, 84
Sissons, Jeffrey, 13
Sitting Bull, 81
  See also Battle of Little Bighorn; Custer
Slice, Barbara, 51
Small, Christopher, 4, 30, 76
Smith, Paul Chaat, 77, 78, 104
Smoke Signals (Eyre), 1
Society of American Indians (SAI), 77
  See also political activism; Red Power
    Movement
Songmakers Round Dance, 41 fig. 2.5
songs
  peyote, 97, 103, 104
  See also pow-wow
Sound of America (SOAR) record label, 107

soundings activism. *See* La Farge; Deloria,
    Vine; political activism; Redbone;
    Sainte-Marie; Westerman; XIT;
Spence, Theresa, 90
Standing Bear, Luther, 97
Standing Rock reservation, 66
"Stardust" (Pettiford), 102
Stone Mountain, 67
Strauss, Neil, 17
Stroud, Robert, 74
Suazo, Jomac, 88
Sweetwater Singers, 28

Tangen, Rulan, 48–51
Taos Pueblo, 73
Tewa, 18
Theisz, R. D., 20, 21, 23. 25
Thinking Musically (Wade), 3
Thom, Mel, 78
time
    visual representation of circular, 7 fig. 1.2
    visual representation of linear, 6 fig. 1.1
Title IV Indian Education Project, 45, 51
Tom Ware and Blues Nation, 65
Toppah, Ernest, 36
Trail of Broken Treaties, 77, 78
*Treasury of Library of Congress Field Recordings,
    A*, 65
Treaty of Canandaigua, 84
Treaty of Fort Laramie, 80–81
    See also Custer, Battle of Little Bighorn
tribal areas
    in Alaska, map of, xxiv, 11
    in Canada, map of, xxv, 11
    in United States, map of, xxiii, 11
Tribe Called Red, A, 90
    "Road, The," 90
tribes. *See* specific names of tribes
Troutman, John, 97
Truth and Reconciliation Commission, 105
*Tunes for 'Toons: Music and the Hollywood
    Cartoon* (Goldmark), 93
Two World Concerto (DeMars), 71, 72

Ute, 56, 68

Valdez-Mor, Miguel, 49
Vanguard Records, 82
Vegas, Lolly. *See* Redbone
Vegas, Pat. *See* Redbone

Velie, 77
Vennum, Thomas, 20
    construction of drums, 25

Wade, Bonnie C., 4
    Thinking Musically, 3
Waldron, Mal, 104
Wapp, Edward R.
    and flute music, 62, 64, 65, 67
Wappo, 74
War Party, 3, 90
    Resistance, The, 90
Warjack, LaNada, 80
Warner Bros. studios, 95
Warrior, Clyde, 78
Warrior, Robert 77, 78
Westerman, Floyd Red Crow, 75, 76
    image, 85 fig. 4.2
    Custer Died for Your Sins, 84–86
"We've Got Blue Skies" (Jackson 5), 88
whistles. *See* flutes
White, Glen H., 36
Whiteman, Paul, 98
Wintun, 74
"Witchi Tai To," 103, 104
Wounded Knee
    massacre, 20
    II occupation, 77, 78, 88
Wright-McLeod, Brian, 84, 88, 98, 99, 101

XIT, 76, 88–89, 91, 107
    "Coming of the Whiteman, The" 88
    "End?," 88, 89
    image, 89 fig. 4.3
    Original XIT Boyz, The, 88
    Plight of the Redman, 88

Yaqui, 86
Yavapai, 77
Yellow Thunder, Raymond, 78
Young Bear, Severt , 20, 21, 23, 25
Young Bird Singers, 37
Young, Gloria, 9
Youngblood, Mary, 57, 71–73
    Aleut Story, 72
    and the block flute, 72
    Beneath the Raven Moon, 72
    Dance with the Wind, 72
    Grammy awards, 72, 107
Yup'ik, 73